PRAISE FOR
He Loves Me!

"Understanding God's love requires not a classroom lecture but a long bath. In HE LOVES ME! Wayne Jacobsen fills the tub and invites us to soak in real life, the inner life of the Trinity. 'What Really Happened on the Cross?' is worth reading five or six times, then sinking quietly and deeply into its life-giving water."
—Dr. Larry Crabb, author of *The Papa Prayer* and *SoulTalk*

"For those of us who are longing to 'live loved,' I cannot recommend a better follow-up to *The Shack* than this book. It is an exploration and adventure into the heart of the God we hoped was truly there, and who loves each of us in particular with an everlasting love."
—Wm. Paul Young, author of *The Shack*

"HE LOVES ME! is one of those rare books in life that frees you to walk with the Father like never before. Its lessons become a part of your journey and stay with you for life like a good friend."
—Bobby Downes, Christiancinema.com

"This book is a refreshing alternative to all the religious stuff available! A heartwarming read that sets you free to receive Jesus' wonderful grace and love."
—John Langford, Hislife.co.uk, Bournemouth, England

"This is my number one book recommendation for anyone struggling with guilt, shame, or the burden of religion. Besides the Scriptures themselves, I have seen this book touch more lives (including my own) than any other book in print."
—Arnie Boedecker, Cornerstone Books

"When I read this book something in the deepest part of me calls out, 'This is the truth.' It is as if I've always known it yet could never have given expression to such things or experienced them. What is written here fuels deep desire and makes living in the Father's love not just possible but absolutely essential. If I could, I would give a copy to everyone I know!"
—Nina Rice, Dublin, Ireland

"After reading the chapter 'The Most Powerful Force in the Universe,' I said to my wife, 'This chapter alone is worth twice the price of the book!' My wife and I have distributed this book throughout New England and the feedback from both old and new believers has been terrific."
—Jack Gerry, Crossroads Ministry

"My husband and I are so blessed by the message of HE LOVES ME! In the past three years I have been on a journey of discovering the heart of God and His amazing love that has so changed me. Thank you for your book."
—Cheryl Haley, pastor

"After [I'd been] a Christian for over twenty years, and in 'ministry' for over ten, HE LOVES ME! revolutionized my walk with the Lord! I repented and rejoiced all through the book. I take it to Africa on every trip. I teach from it, I give it as a gift, and I fill up personally when I begin to backslide into my religiosity."
—Penny Dugan, New Jerusalem Mission

"In HE LOVES ME! Wayne Jacobsen's incredible ability to communicate allows us to share his experience of the God who is love. In words that give the reader a glimpse of the Father with clarity and passion, he overcomes the picture that years of religion have clouded."
—Kevin Smith, Australia

"Have you ever felt as though you've failed God? This book will make you want to climb into Father's lap and stay there. Wayne's thought-provoking words passionately disarm the idea that the Father's love for his children is in any way attached to their performance. A fresh and stunning look at the cross of Christ brings the message home."
—Dave Fredrickson, Family Room Media

"It appears that the only way we can get our needs met for unconditional love and a feeling of worth is to depend on what others think of us. But once we realize that we are loved by the Father, we are free—free from having to control and manipulate others to accept us. This book is the most freeing message I have ever read as [I] understand that God really, really loves [me]."
—Dave Coleman, retired hospice chaplain

"I took up the book with some reservations but was bowled over by the powerful revelation of grace and love that forms the foundation of Wayne's thinking. The book confirmed deep truths about how much He loves me and how far I drifted off into the land of religion and effort."
—Stephan Vosloo, Ladysmith, South Africa

"This book was a foundational part of the changes the Father has worked in me over the past several years to reshape my understanding of God. I encourage you to read it with great expectancy of what the Father can accomplish within the relationship He has always wanted with you."
—Kent Burgess, Faithfully Dangerous, St. Louis, Missouri

Other Books by Wayne Jacobsen

Tales of the Vine

In My Father's Vineyard

Authentic Relationships (with Clay Jacobsen)

*So You Don't Want to Go
to Church Anymore* (with Dave Coleman)

The Shack (in collaboration with
author Wm. Paul Young)

He Loves Me!

Learning to Live in the Father's Affection

WAYNE JACOBSEN

windblown
MEDIA
Newbury Park, CA

He Loves Me! by Wayne Jacobsen
Second Edition

International Standard Book Number
978-0-9647292-5-4

Copyright © 2007 by Wayne Jacobsen
All rights reserved

Published in association with Hachette Book Group USA.

10   9   8   7

Windblown Media, 4680 Calle Norte,
Newbury Park, CA 91320 • office@windblownmedia.com
(805) 498-2484; (805) 499-4260 (fax)

Printed in the United States of America

To Sara,

On the celebration of our
twenty-fifth
wedding anniversary

I couldn't have found a better
friend or beloved partner with
whom I could share this journey.
Your example of loving me
through my worst moments and
laying down your life at great
personal sacrifice has taught
me more about God's love and
how I can trust him freely than
anyone else on the planet.

Contents

I. THE RELATIONSHIP GOD HAS ALWAYS WANTED WITH YOU

II. WHAT FEAR COULD NEVER ACHIEVE

III. THE UNDENIABLE PROOF

IV. A LIFE LIVED IN LOVE

Foreword

With wise words and thorough logic, Wayne Jacobsen leaves no obstacle standing between a believer and God the Father. He carefully and gently pushes aside any resistance to absolute reliance on the grace of God and his plan for us. Some journeys carry such dangers and mysteries that we long for a hand to hold and a secure face to see. This book places your hand in the secure one and clearly portrays the face of God.

When Jesus answered a questioner and informed him (and us) that the greatest commandment was to "love God with all your heart, soul, mind and strength," for many of us, this was a command to which we could only aspire. Perhaps we even prayed, "Lord, I want to love you with all my heart, soul, mind, and strength." After reading this book, I am confident you will easily say, "I do love you completely."

No matter what your emotional state, peace will settle on your heart. Any anxieties about God are going to fade. Prepare your face for a smile and your heart for a constant parade of brass bands celebrating a great victory.

As you read and receive the understanding of this book, you will frequent God's presence much more because the eternal relationship you will find there is so superior to your own best efforts or dreams. These gifts of God are unattainable on your own, but you will find this book to be an invitation to God's house and its warmth with an RSVP. With that invitation in hand, you will feel as if you have "arrived"—and you have!

If it seems that I push too hard and compliment this book too highly, it is on purpose. You hold in your hands a classic.

Be prepared to know God better and love him more. You are about to go on a journey whose road map you will save for repeat use and whose copies you will gladly and freely give to others.

—GAYLE D. ERWIN
Author, *Jesus Style*

Introduction
to the Second Edition

I've been amazed at how far and wide this little book has gone since it was first printed eight years ago. I have often said since then that I would never write a more significant book, and I'm even more convinced of that today.

I realize that a book about God's love seems so obvious that most people would rather plow on to seemingly more engaging subjects, such as New Testament church models, more effective ways to pray, or keys to living in God's will. God's love seems like Christianity 101 to most people. "Let's get on to the deeper things," they'll say. But there is nothing deeper.

Certainly there is nothing more theologically certain than that God is love. We sing about his love in our simplest songs and are comfortable with using the language of love as it relates to God. But in a practical sense, incredibly few believers live each day as if the God of the universe has great affection for them.

Why? Because two thousand years of religious tradition have inculcated in us the mistaken notion that God's love is something we earn. If we do what pleases him, he loves us; if not, he doesn't. Giving that up isn't easy. Moving from a performance-based religious ethic to a relationship deeply rooted in the Father's affection is no small transition. It is the most significant one I've ever made in my spiritual journey, and it changed my life in Christ from a frustrating drudgery in the face of enticing temptations to a vital, fulfilling adventure that continues to transform me with each passing day. This book describes that process for me, and I hope it can help others in that transition as well.

Some years ago I was asked by a group of elders to teach a nine-week series at a local congregation while they were between pastors. When I asked them if they had anything specific in mind, they told me they had heard I was teaching some fresh things about the cross and would love to hear those. (You'll find most of that content in these pages.) I was concerned about doing so, since I knew the freedom of that teaching could undermine what most congregations use to manipulate people to get involved and serve.

"Let me ask you a question first," I responded. "Just how much do you think gets done around here because people would feel guilty if they didn't do it?"

I was surprised when one of the men answered, with a laugh and a shake of his head, "Probably 90 percent!" The others laughed, too, but in the end they agreed that it might be something like that.

"Well, if you're right," I told them, "and if your people have a revelation of the cross, then 90 percent of what's getting done around here will stop. I want to know if you're okay with that."

The laughter ceased. They looked at one another, unsure how to respond. After some hemming and hawing, they finally agreed that they would be fine with that. You've got to admire their courage. So I agreed to come.

Unfortunately, however, that was not the outcome. Either I didn't teach it well or they didn't listen as well as I hoped, because at the end of our time, they hired a new pastor who came talking the language of guilt and performance. I was saddened that the group as a whole didn't seem to catch on, though I am still in touch today with some of the individuals in that group who were deeply transformed.

The pull of religion can be far stronger than the freedom of relationship. I can't tell you how many times I've shared these things only to be faced with people who honestly believe that

God's love alone is not able to transform people. Instead, they argue, we have to give them a hefty and consistent dose of God's fear and judgment to keep them on the straight and narrow.

It's tragic really. Those who are willing to substitute the demand of obligation for the power of affection have not tasted the latter in any significant measure. I have observed all over the world that those who discover the depth of the Father's affection for them and learn to live in it find greater passion for Jesus and freedom from sin and are more engaged with the world than anyone driven by religious obligation.

What the Father showed us in the gift of his Son is that he was unwilling to settle for the indentured servitude of fearful slaves. He preferred instead the intimate affection of sons and daughters. He knew love would take us deeper into his life than fearful obligation ever would. It would teach us more truth, free us from our selfishness and failures, and make us fruitful in the world.

Since I published this book I've heard from hundreds of people who have told me that God used it to transform their own journeys as well. Many told me that I had put into words something they knew deep inside was already true, but they were afraid to believe it. Others have said it completely redefined the life of Christ for them and sent them on an amazing journey mining the depths of that love and affection.

I hope you, too, come to the end of these pages convinced that he loves you with a deep and unrelenting affection. Nothing fulfills his purpose more than when his love overwhelms you, then transforms you, and then leads you through the rest of your life as a reflection of his glory in the earth.

That's why he made you, and I hope why this book has landed in your hands.

—Wayne Jacobsen
August 2007

SECTION I

The Relationship God Has Always Wanted with You

On that day you will realize that
I am in my Father, and you are in me,
and I am in you.

—John 14:20

He loves me.
He loves me not.
He loves me.
He loves me not.

Daisy-Petal Christianity

THE LITTLE GIRL STANDS in the backyard chanting as she plucks petals one by one from the daisy and drops them to the ground. At game's end, the last petal tells all: whether or not the person desired returns the affection.

Of course no one takes it seriously, and if children don't get the answer they desire, they take another daisy and start again. It doesn't take long even for children to realize that flowers weren't designed to tell romantic fortunes. Why should they link their hearts' desires to the fickleness of chance?

Why indeed! But it is a lesson far easier learned in romance than in more spiritual pursuits. For long after we've put away our daisies, many of us continue to play the game with God. This time we don't pluck flower petals but probe through our circumstances trying to figure out exactly how God feels about us.

> I got a raise. *He loves me.*
> I didn't get the promotion I wanted; I lost my job altogether. *He loves me not!*
> Something in the Bible inspired me today. *He loves me!*
> My child is seriously ill. *He loves me not!*
> I gave money to someone in need. *He loves me!*
> I let my anger get the best of me. *He loves me not!*
> Something for which I prayed actually happened. *He loves me!*
> I stretched the truth to get myself out of a tight spot. *He loves me not!*
> A friend called me unexpectedly to encourage me. *He loves me!*
> My car needs a new transmission. *He loves me not!*

A PERILOUS TIGHTROPE

I have played that game most of my life, trying to sort out in any given moment how God might feel about me personally. I grew up learning that he is a God of love, and for the most part I believed it to be true.

In good times, nothing is easier to believe. On days when my family is healthy and our relationships a joy, when my ministry thrives and both income and opportunity increase, when we have plenty of time to enjoy our friends and are not burdened with need, who wouldn't be certain of God's love?

But that certainty erodes when those times of bliss are interrupted with more troublesome events

> A childhood condition that provided no end of embarrassment.

The day one of my friends in high school died of a brain tumor even as we prayed earnestly for his healing.

When I wasn't selected for a job I wanted in college because someone had lied about me.

The night my house was robbed.

When I was severely burned in a kitchen accident.

When I watched my father-in-law and my brother both die with debilitating illnesses even though they sought God earnestly for healing.

When colleagues in ministry lied to me and spread false stories about me to win the support of others.

When I didn't know from where my next paycheck would come.

When I saw my wife crushed by circumstances that I couldn't get God to change, no matter how hard I tried.

When doors of opportunity that appeared certain to open would suddenly slam shut like a windblown door.

Then I wondered how God really felt about me. I couldn't understand how a God who loved me either would allow such things into my life or wouldn't fix them immediately so that I or people I loved wouldn't have to endure such pain.

He loves me not! Or so I thought on those days. My disappointment with God could easily turn two directions. Often in my pain and frustration, when I felt as if I had done enough to deserve better, I would rail at God like the Job of old, accusing him of being either unfair or unloving.

In more honest moments, however, I was well aware of the temptations and failures that could exclude me from his care. I would come out of those times committed to trying harder to live the life I thought would merit his love.

I lived for thirty-four years as a believer on this perilous tightrope. Even when there was no crisis hanging over my head, I was always wary of the next one God might drop on me at any second if I couldn't stay on his good side. In some ways I had become like the schizophrenic child of an abusive father, never certain what God I'd meet on any given day—the one who wanted to scoop me up in his arms with laughter, or the one who would ignore me or punish me for reasons I could never understand.

Only in the last twelve years have I discovered that my methods of discerning God's love were as flawed as pulling petals from a daisy. I haven't been the same since.

CONVINCING EVIDENCE

What about you?

Have you ever felt tossed back and forth by circumstances, occasionally certain but mostly uncertain about how the Creator of the universe feels about you? Or perhaps you've never even known how much God loves you.

In a Bible study recently, I met a forty-year-old woman who was active in her fellowship but admitted to a small group of us that she had never been certain that God loved her. She seemed to want to tell me more but finally only asked me to pray for her.

As I did, asking God to reveal just how much he loved her, an image came to mind. I saw a figure I knew to be Jesus walking through a meadow hand in hand with a little girl about five years old. Somehow I knew this woman was that little girl. I prayed that he would help her discover a childlikeness of spirit that would allow her to skip through the meadows with him.

When I finished praying I looked up at her eyes, brimming with tears.

"Did you say 'meadow'?" she asked.

I nodded, thinking it odd she had focused on that word.

Immediately she began to cry. When she was able to speak, she said, "I wasn't sure I wanted to tell you. When I was five years old I was molested in a meadow by an older boy. Whenever I think about God, I think about that horrible event and I wonder why, if he loved me so much, he didn't stop that from happening."

She's not alone. Many people carry scars and disappointments that appear to be convincing evidence that the God of love does not exist or, if he does, he maintains a safe distance from them and leaves them to the whim of other people's sins.

I don't have a stock answer for moments like that, as if any could be effective in the midst of such pain. I told her that evidently God wanted her to know he had been there with her, and although he didn't act in the only way she could understand true love to act, he loved her nonetheless. He wanted to walk her through that defiled meadow and redeem it in her life.

He wanted to give her a measure of joy in the face of the most traumatic event of her life and turn what had destroyed her ability to trust into a stepping-stone toward grace. I know that can sound almost trite in the face of such incredible pain, but the process has begun for her. Eight months later I received an excited e-mail from her telling me in 270-point type, "I get it!"

Does that mean she understands why it happened to her? Of course not. Nothing could explain that. But it does mean that God's love was big enough to contain that horrible event and walk her out of it. It is my hope these words will encourage that process in you as well.

PERCEPTION VERSUS REALITY

Truly God has never acted toward us in any way other than with a depth of love that defies human understanding. I know it may not look like that at times. When he seems to callously disregard our most noble prayers, our trust in him can be easily shattered and we wonder if he cares for us. We can even come up with a list of our own failures that seemingly justify God's indifference and beckon us into a dark whirlpool of self-loathing.

When we're playing the he-loves-me-he-loves-me-not game, the evidence against God can appear overwhelming. For reasons we will probe throughout these pages, God does not often do the things we think his love would compel him to do for us. He often seems to stand by with indifference while we suffer. How often does he seem to disappoint our most noble expectations?

But perception is not necessarily reality. If we define God only in our limited interpretation of our own circumstances, we will never discover who he really is.

He has provided a far better way. Our daisy-petal approach to Christianity can be swallowed up by the undeniable proof of his love for us on the cross of Calvary. That's the side of the cross that has all but been ignored in recent decades. We did not see what really happened there between the Father and his Son that opened the door to his love so vast and so certain that it cannot be challenged even by our darkest days.

Through that door we can really know who God is and embrace a relationship with him that our deepest hearts have hungered to experience. That is where we'll begin, because it is only in the context of the relationship God desires with us that we can discover the full glory of his love.

He does love you more deeply than you've ever imagined; he has done so throughout your entire life. Once you embrace that truth, your troubles will never again drive you to question God's affection for you or whether you've done enough to merit it. Instead of fearing he has turned his back on you, you will be able to trust his love at the moments you need him most. You will even see how that love can flow out of you in the strangest ways to touch a world starved for it.

Learning to trust him like that is not something any of us can resolve in an instant; it's something we'll grow to discover for the whole of our lives. God knows how difficult it is for us to accept his love, and he teaches us with more patience than we've ever known. Through every circumstance and in the most surprising ways, he makes his love known to us in ways we can understand.

So perhaps it's time to toss your daisies aside and discover that it is not the fear of losing God's love that will keep you on his path, but the simple joy of living in it every day.

On the day you discover that, you will truly begin to live!

> *How great is the love the Father has lavished on us, that we should be called children of God! And that is what we are!*
>
> —1 JOHN 3:1

For Your Personal Journey

How often do you find yourself doubting God's love for you? When do you question his love the most? How certain are you that God loves you as deeply as he does anyone else in the world? When difficulties arise, do you find yourself doubting God's love for you or trying to be more righteous so he'll like you more? Ask God in the days ahead to reveal the depths of his love for you.

For Group Discussion

1. Share an experience you went through in which you really doubted if God cared about you.

2. How do you feel about it now? If you're still unsure, what might you ask God to do to change your perception of that event?

3. If you look back now and know that God loved you even if you didn't recognize it at the time, what did you learn in the process?

4. How can we encourage one another to be certain, instead of doubtful, about God's love?

*God is not mute:
the Word spoke,
not out of a
whirlwind, but
out of the human
larynx of a
Palestinian Jew.*

PHILIP YANCEY, *THE JESUS I
NEVER KNEW*

What Jesus' Disciples Didn't Know

CAN YOU IMAGINE what it must have been like for Jesus the first moment he sat in the circle of his disciples after they had finally become friends?

We all know what it takes to get acquainted with new people, the awkward pauses and measured words as people get to know one another. Certainly the disciples went through that with Jesus. Just who was this Teacher and Miracle-worker, and who were these other men who decided to follow him?

It might have happened during a conversation after a meal, or walking together on a road, but at some point they found themselves safe enough with him and one another to let down their guards. No longer measuring words or trying to impress one another, they slipped into the fruits of their burgeoning friendship—the freedom to be honest, to laugh, to ask the seemingly stupid question, and to relax in one another's presence.

What must that have felt like to Jesus? Had this been what he had always wanted?

For the first time since that cruel day in Eden, God was sitting down with people he loved and they were not cowering in fear.

For centuries men and women had stood at a great distance from God, shamed by their sin and intimidated by his holiness. With only a few notable exceptions, people wanted nothing to do with the immediacy of God's presence. When Mount Sinai shook with thunder and earthquakes, the people begged Moses to go to God for them. God was a terrifying figure, and feeling safe with him was unthinkable.

But God had never thought so. He was unfolding his plan to restore the fellowship with humanity that Adam and Eve had lost in their fall. In Jesus, he was able to sit down in the company of those he loved, and they were comfortable enough to engage him in a real conversation. What an incredible moment that must have been for Jesus, to be with people who were not so awed by him that they could not enjoy his presence.

Of course, it happened only because the disciples had no idea that it was God who stoked the fire as they sat around and laughed. For although we now know that Jesus was God incarnate on Earth, they had no idea, and that made all the difference.

GOD IN DISGUISE

I like arriving early at places where I'm supposed to speak so that I can meet the people who've invited me and still have time to mingle among the gathering crowd. I introduce myself only by my first name and never let on that I'm the speaker.

Surprisingly few people ever figure it out, and so I get to engage in real conversations with the people before I speak.

I've learned that people treat me differently before they learn I'm the speaker or the author from out of town. They are so much more themselves, willing to talk freely about their lives and their aspirations. Once they find out who I am, all of that changes. They are far more self-conscious and inhibited, preferring to focus questions on me and my work. The level of fellowship I enjoy most with people is destroyed after my identity is revealed.

Admittedly, it might be a bit misleading. I've watched people near me cringe with embarrassment when I'm finally introduced. Some even come up afterward and apologize for not realizing who I was and for "going on" about their children or their work, as if those things have just become trivial because of who I am. But I remind them that I was the one who asked and wouldn't have done so if I wasn't interested.

Once people put me in the guest speaker box, it is hard for me to climb out. It usually takes a long time for people to relax and let me be the brother in Christ I really am. As confining as the guest speaker role can be for me, I suspect the box into which people put God is vastly worse for him. So I understand why he had to take on a disguise to have the relationship with people he had always desired.

The disciples were in the physical presence of God and were completely unaware of it. They knew he was a man of God, of course. Who could watch his miracles and listen to his wisdom without knowing that?

On at least one occasion they identified him as the Messiah, but there was nothing in the first-century Jewish hope of the Messiah that expected God to be incarnate in human flesh. They expected him to be a man, empowered by God as was Moses, David, or Elijah. But the idea that God would take on human flesh and live that way on Earth would have been unthinkable.

How could the holy God live among sinful people and engage them face-to-face? Their history told of such moments when God's presence came to his people. Even the most righteous had fallen on their faces in fear, and some of the most evil had died. They thought that's what God wanted, but as we'll see their response had far more to do with how sinful people reacted to God than how God wanted to be known.

THE UNVEILING

So God disguised himself, first as a baby in a manger, then as a young boy growing up in Nazareth, and finally as a young man walking the hills of Galilee. No one had any idea God had come to live among them; because of that no one cowered in fear or acted awkwardly with him.

For the first time since he walked the Garden with Adam and Eve, God was among people the way he had always wanted to be. People with broken lives were drawn to him, not repelled. His followers were secure enough in his presence to be genuine, even when that revealed lust for power or arrogance. Now God could experience the relationship he'd always wanted with his people and through that relationship free them from sin.

Not even in the last day of Jesus' life before he was crucified had the disciples figured out who he really was. Jesus said as much during the last meal he ate with them. "If you really knew me, you would know my Father as well." When Philip questioned him on it, certain he had no idea who his Father was, Jesus got even clearer: "Don't you know me . . . even after I have been among you such a long time? Anyone who has seen me has seen the Father. How can you say, 'Show us the Father'?" (John 14:7–9).

But now he wanted them to know. The disguise was about to come off. "Don't you believe that I am in the Father, and that the Father is in me?" In a few hours he would be taken from them, tried, tortured, and executed. The next time the disciples would see him he would be the resurrected Christ. There would be no hiding who he really was.

How would the disciples treat him then? Would they resort to cowering away in terror of his majesty? Jesus didn't want that realization to destroy the relationship he'd cultivated with them but to make it grow even stronger.

His words in the upper room were designed to help them

move the relationship they had experienced with Jesus in the flesh to the Father they didn't yet know, to the postresurrected Christ, and to the Holy Spirit. Instead of being with them in the flesh, however, God would come and dwell within. Not only could the relationship continue there, Jesus told them it would be even better than they had already experienced with him: "On that day you will realize that I am in my Father, and you are in me, and I am in you" (John 14:20).

Read those words again. Having just told them that he and the Father were one because the Father was in him, he then invited them into that same relationship. *You will be in me and I will be in you.*

In these simple words Jesus revealed what God's desire had been from the first day of creation: to invite men and women into the relationship that God has known with himself for all eternity. It is as if they could not keep to themselves the joy, love, glory, and trust that they had always shared together. Their purpose in creating the world was to invite us as mere creations to share the wonder of that relationship.

TENDER IMAGES

The friendship Jesus shared with his disciples was the model for the relationship he extends to you. He wants to be the voice that steers you through every situation, the peace that sets your troubled heart at rest, and the power that holds you up in the storm. He wants to be closer than your dearest friend and more faithful than any other person you've ever known.

I know it sounds preposterous. How can mere humans enjoy such a friendship with the almighty God who created with a word all we see? Do I dare think he would know and care about the details of my life? Isn't it presumptuous even to imagine that this God would take delight in me, even though I still struggle with the failures of my flesh?

It would be so if this were not his idea. He's the one who offered to be your loving Father—sharing life with you in ways no earthly father ever could.

Don't relegate this invitation to an abstract spiritual plane. When Scripture talks about the relationship God wants with us, it borrows the most tender images of our world. Scripture describes us as young children beloved by a gracious Father, the bride of an expectant bridegroom, friends dear enough to die for, and little chicks rushing under the protective wings of a hen.

He is obviously serious about the intimacy and security of a relationship with him built on love and trust. Many shy away from such thoughts, feeling they demean the transcendence of the almighty God. To be honest, their fears are often fulfilled in those who feign a chumminess with God that distorts who he really is.

But we must not let an abuse of others keep us from the reality God offers us. As we shall see, finding a true friendship with the living God never demeans who he is. It doesn't reduce him to our level and allow us to treat him tritely; it only defines his Fatherhood in ever more grandeur.

The fact that my earthly father extends to me his friendship does not diminish his fatherhood. It only defines it more clearly. I am his friend, and I give him respect as my father. In the same way, God wants us to trust his love so that we can be secure in his presence. But it is still the presence of the living God that makes this friendship all the more incredible.

To experience it, however, we need to appreciate just how much we are loved. That isn't easy for a generation of believers who have been invited to know him not because he is so overwhelmingly wonderful, but because we were scared to death by the threat of an eternity in hell. We will look at that in the next chapter.

> *I no longer call you servants, because a servant does not know his master's business. Instead, I have called you friends, for everything that I learned from my Father I have made known to you.*
>
> —JOHN 15:15

For Your Personal Journey

Spend a few moments thinking about your relationship with God. Do you see it growing in closeness and sensitivity, or does it feel abstract? Is he more real than your closest friend, or a distant presence that rarely seems to engage in the real issues of your life? If your relationship with him isn't what you want it to be, ask him to help you grow to know him better and to recognize his presence throughout each day.

For Group Discussion

1. Share your favorite Bible story of God's revealing himself to someone.

2. What do you see in the relationship Jesus had with his disciples that you want to see in your own relationship with him?

3. Share an experience from your own life when you knew God's presence was with you in some tangible way.

4. Spend a few moments talking about what you can do to grow to know God better.

*The Satanic assumption
is that men and women
cannot love God for his
own sake.*

DAVID BOAN AND JOHN YATES,
UNPUBLISHED MANUSCRIPT

Threatened with Hell

THE QUESTION IS COMPELLING. "Do you know where you would end up if you died in a car accident tonight?"

The evangelist has already painted the pictures. You could find yourself in an eternal garden of exquisite beauty laced together with winding paths of gold—or writhing in agony amid the leaping sulfuric flames of hell.

If there was ever a choice that defined "no-brainer," this is it. Once you convince someone that hell and heaven exist, winning a convert is easy. After all, praying for forgiveness and "accepting Jesus" seem like a small price to pay for a get-out-of-hell-free card!

So effective is this appeal to people's worst fears and inse-curities that hell has become the most popular invitation into God's kingdom. What we have not so critically examined is whether or not threatening people with hell engages them in the relationship God has always wanted with them.

We live in a day when millions of people have made a com-mitment to Christ and yet few lives are really transformed by his power. It has been said of this generation that our Christianity is a mile wide but only an inch deep. We see effects of it everywhere. People claim to know God but show no evi-dence of transformation in their daily lives. We challenge them as hypocrites and attempt to badger them into more-righteous lifestyles, but in the end most believers end up as much a part of the world's ways as their nonbelieving neighbors.

While the threat of hell can stir instant commitments, it does not breed long-term disciples. If you are in this king-dom only because you fear the alternative, you've missed the greatest part of what it means to know God.

WHY THE THREAT?

No one ever threatened to do something that was won-derful. My parents didn't threaten me with punishment to get me to go to Disneyland. But to make me go to the den-tist or work on the vineyard, that was another matter.

So if I am told that I must love God or he will throw me into hell, I might well consider loving him—or at least pre-tend I do. But if the only reason I'm even responding to him is to serve my own self-interest and escape a fiery eternity in hell, am I really loving him or myself?

Can a true friendship blossom under so grave a threat? Let's say I approach a recent acquaintance of mine, hoping to deepen our friendship. I say to him, "I have really appreciated the time we've been able to spend together. In fact, I'd like to see our relationship grow and maybe even become best friends. How would you like to spend some time together over the next few months and see if that kind of friendship develops?"

So far, so good! But what if I added one more sentence: "I hope you do, because if you don't, I'm going to hunt you down and torture you for the rest of your life." Hasn't the invitation just taken an ominous turn? Even if he wanted to explore the potential of a friendship with me, it has now been twisted by my threat. What does that say about me? How will he ever feel safe in a friendship cultivated on fear?

Whether we are conscious of it or not, the threat of hell can create an inner dissonance in our perception of the God who seeks our love. How can we feel safe with a God who is seemingly anxious to dangle us over the flames of hell? If he can find nothing else to call us to him, then what kind of God must he be? And if we can find no better reason to love him, how shallow must our faith be?

Fifteen years ago, a full-page advertisement in a popular Christian leadership magazine quoted a popular television pastor:

> *If God would dip all pastors in hell for a fraction of a second and then yank them up by their shirttails—as they are standing there smoldering, and their clothes and skin are full of black soot, and their shoes have half melted off—I think their commitment to the Great Commission would substantially increase.*

Sadly, he's probably right, but that may point more to our weakness than to God's intentions. The threat of hell may get people to evangelize more, to repeat a sinner's prayer, or even to join a congregation, but in doing so it gives a sordid view of God as one who delights in searing the soles of our shoes in order to get us to do things his way. Such a view of him will not invite us into the depths of his love.

CONTRADICTORY PORTRAITS?

This is the problem, isn't it? Scripture seems to paint two contradictory portraits of the living God: a terrible Judge and a loving Father. Which is it? Can he be both?

We read not only that God has prepared hell for the non-believing, but also that he commanded Joshua to practice ethnic cleansing in Canaan, poured out fire from heaven to consume Sodom and Gomorrah, and opened the earth to swallow those who opposed Moses. God was so unapproachable in his purity, even the most righteous fell on their faces near his presence, paralyzed by their unworthiness. He demanded unquestioning obedience and punished those who did not comply with unspeakable anguish.

No wonder we're at least a little confused when he appears in the New Testament and tells us how much he loves us and invites us to be his children. We saw Jesus healing the sick, forgiving prostitutes and murderers, going into the houses of sinners. He invited children into his lap and portrayed his Father as so tender that the most wayward sinner could run to his side in absolute safety.

So what happened to God? Did he get "saved" somewhere between Malachi and Matthew? Had he reinvented himself into a nicer, gentler God? Of course not! He is unchanging, the same throughout all eternity.

So, then, is he both? Is he kind and gentle to those who please him and vengeful toward the wicked? That's what many of us have been taught to believe, which is why we end up playing he-loves-me-he-loves-me-not games. We sift through every event to try to figure out if we are in his favor or out of it. If we think we are in, we can relax and coast through life. If, however, we think our difficulties prove we are out of favor, we have to try harder to please him—a course of action Paul warns us against. True righteousness cannot come from human effort.

There's the problem. I can't please him until I'm certain of his love for me, but he will not love me if I cannot please him. This is an endless loop that offers no resolution. How can he be a mean and vengeful God one moment and a kind and tender one the next? Those portraits don't depict the same God in different circumstances, but rather two contradictory natures of God that leave us confused and uncertain.

Unless we can glean from Scripture a cohesive view of

God's nature, we'll never know who he really is or have the confidence to embrace the relationship he desires with us. God did not change between Malachi and Matthew. Our perception of him, however, changed drastically.

Before Jesus came we could see only God's actions and assume he was moved by motivations similar to our own. His actions against sin made him appear as if he didn't care for people. His attempts to teach his people to trust him were misunderstood as vengeful punishment.

Jesus changed all of that. By listening to his words and watching how he lived, we suddenly see God's motivations. He fully reflected the Father's glory so we might know him as he really is and no longer be victims of our own misinterpretations. Love dwells at the core of God's being, and the Old Testament contains hundreds of pictures of a God who is rich in mercy, willing to forgive, and passionate about setting us free from the sin that diminishes and devours the life he wants us to experience in him.

He allows us the consequences of sin, not because he delights in our anguish, but so that we can see its devastating effects and run to the only one in the universe who can set us free from them. His wrath against sin was not his rejection of us in anger, but only a reflection of the depth of his love that cannot look away unconcerned as sin destroys us.

These are not mere philosophical issues. If we aren't certain of God's motives toward us, we will never have confidence to engage his presence in the reality of our lives. We'll keep him at a safe distance and miss what he desires most for us: a friendship with him more real and more powerful than any we've known before.

"DO I HAVE TO?"

Those who seek to follow God only because they don't want to go to hell never discover how incredible a Father he really is. They see Christianity as an onerous burden and don't want to do one bit more than they absolutely must.

I've heard the question literally hundreds of times. Struggling with sin or desiring something that Scripture marks as out of bounds for the believer, they'll ask what I think they should do. When I tell them what Scripture seems to say, I see the look in their eyes—gears are turning as they feverishly try to find a loophole so they can still have what they desire and not end up in hell.

From the lips of a woman wanting to marry a man who doesn't share her faith: "Do I have to, to be saved?"

From the angry man who doesn't want to forgive the person who cheated him: "Do I have to, to be saved?"

From the person who wants to justify the habit God wants to free him from: "Do I have to, to be saved?"

How does one answer that question? If you say yes, then you empty the cross of its power by substituting human effort. If you say no, they will use it as an excuse to indulge themselves in a false notion of what it means to live in God.

The question itself is unfair and shows how far removed Christianity has become from its central purpose. Instead of desiring to walk in friendship with him, we are only preoccupied with securing his goodies. It's his blessing we want, not him! How painful that must be for him.

It would be as if I invited my adult son over to dinner some Friday evening. He hesitates a moment. It's obvious he'd rather not come, but before he answers he wants to know one thing: "Dad, I guess I could come, but I've got other things I'd like to do. Will you write me out of your will if I don't come?"

What answer can a father give to that question? None would really suffice, since the question misses the whole point of relationship. True, God has the best goodies in all the universe, but the person who seeks those without desiring to know him misses out on the real life of the kingdom.

That's what people are saying who wonder if they must do something or risk losing their salvation. They don't want one drop more of God's life than the minimum required to escape hell. How tragic! No wonder they missed the best gift God could give them. Jesus wanted desperately to free them from the tyranny of trying to earn eternal life by their own religious efforts.

All this is not to say that hell does not exist, or that dire consequences await those who refuse God's freedom. What I am saying is that when we use the threat of hell to motivate people to come to God, we are using it in a way Jesus never did and in a way he never intended. In doing so, we push people farther away from God's greatest desire rather than inviting them closer to it.

His message was not "Come to God or you'll burn in hell." His message was "God's kingdom has come near you and you can become a participant in it. You have a Father who loves you more than any other person ever has or ever will, and you can now discover what it means to have a daily relationship with him. If you choose not to, then your own sin will destroy you utterly and completely."

Jesus compared this life to a treasure discovered in a field: something so valuable that you would give up anything to possess it. His life is not something you have to follow. He is worth knowing just because of how incredibly awesome he is. If you want his gifts without wanting him, you cheat yourself out of the best portion.

Here the fear of hell is no use to us at all. The insecurity it breeds only takes us further from him and makes us uncertain about who he is. Jesus wanted us to be very clear about who his Father is because we grow in him only to the degree that we trust his love for us.

There is no one God does not love with all that he is. His love reaches beyond every sin and failure, hoping that at some moment every person will come to know just how loved he or she is.

There is nothing more important for you to know.

The kingdom of heaven is like treasure hidden in a field. When a man found it, he hid it again, and then in his joy went and sold all he had and bought that field.
— MATTHEW 13:44

For Your Personal Journey

Did you come to God only because you were afraid of the alternative, or were you entreated by his love? Do you view him as a stern judge or a loving Father? If the former, ask God to reveal himself to you as he really is. Over the next few weeks, look for ways God will help you let go of your fears. Let his love capture your heart as your sole motivation for walking after him.

For Group Discussion

1. Why do religious people use the threat of hell to get people to come to God?

2. When you think of God appearing in your life, what do you see? How would he act, and what does he feel about you? Would you see Jesus treating you the same way if he showed up? How do we reconcile the two?

3. Think about the relationship that Jesus has offered us with his Father. What might we say to communicate to people who don't know him just what kind of God he is?

4. Ask God to free you from fearing his judgment and teach you instead how to trust his love.

If we take all the goodness, wisdom and compassion of the best mothers and fathers who have ever lived, they would only be a faint shadow of the love and mercy in the heart of the redeeming God.

BRENNAN MANNING, *THE SIGNATURE OF JESUS*

A Father Like No Other

"THE OLD MAN IS A FOOL! And so is my brother. Good riddance to you all!"

If those weren't his words, they at least express his attitude. How he must have cackled in delight that his father had actually given him his share of the inheritance that he had demanded. He was finally free of his father and the hard work of the family farm, too. With more money than he could imagine spending in a lifetime, he walked off to find himself in a world filled with opportunity.

All didn't go as he planned. How quickly his excessive pleasures devoured his money. Then when a severe famine swept his adopted country, he had to use what was left just to survive. But even that ran out eventually, and he had to sell himself into slavery to a master who fed his livestock better than his servants.

One day he found himself coveting the slop tossed to the pigs, and only then did he think of home again. This time he did not loathe it, he longed for it. He had been better off at home. He wondered if it would be possible to go back there again.

Traditionally this story is called "The Parable of the Prodigal Son" and is one of Jesus' most poignant tales. It has been told and retold because it is so easy to identify with the son and the mercy he received in spite of his arrogance and stupidity.

By focusing on the prodigal son, however, we lose the central lesson of the parable. He was only one of two brothers, each dealing with an estrangement from their father, albeit in vastly different ways.

The central character is the father himself, and for that reason I wish it were called "The Parable of the Incredible Father." For Jesus used this story to paint a portrait of his Father, and believe me, this is like no father you've ever known.

WHAT FATHER IS THIS?

Anyone hearing Jesus' story for the first time would be shocked at this father's actions. His arrogant son dishonored him by asking for his inheritance while the father was still alive and by all indications was nowhere near death's door. What kind of son claims his father's inheritance while he's still alive? How dare he even ask!

As rude as the son's request might have been, we can at least understand it. We all know what it is to want to get our hands on Dad's money, even if most of us are too civil to pursue it. But it's this father who defies comprehension.

What did the father do in response to this outrageous request? *He gave it to him.* This is even more shocking than the son asking. He divided the inheritance between his two sons and let him go. How many fathers would do that, especially knowing the younger son was up to no good?

What kind of father was this?

The son squandered his inheritance on his own pleasure instead of investing it for the future. But the father did not nag him. The son finally lost it all and ended up destitute. But the father did not try to rescue him.

Where was the father? He was back on the farm, waiting. He didn't chase after his son to tell him that he was foolish, nor did he rush off to buy him dinner when famine hit. He waited.

What kind of father was this?

Was he indifferent to his son's plight? Parents who have watched their sons or daughters make bad choices know that waiting is far more difficult than prodding or nagging. But wait he did, for a marvelous thing to happen—to let the son come to his senses.

We soon find out, however, just how expectant that waiting was. Years later when the son returned, the father spotted him while he was still a long ways off. The only way that would have happened was if the father had been constantly looking. He probably never walked by the road without looking down it, hoping against hope that today would be the day his boy would come home. I can see him with one eye on his work, the other focused down the road, looking for the familiar gait of his beloved son. One day he spotted him, even though the young man would have been emaciated with hunger and hunched over in humiliation. "That's him! That's my boy!"

What did he do then? Did he stand on the porch with arms crossed, waiting for his son to walk all the way to the house humiliated, then fall down in the dirt and grovel for his next meal? That's what I might have done. I would even have practiced my I-hope-you-learned-your-lesson speech. Not this father.

Without hesitation the father jumped off the porch and ran down the road. This is all the more amazing when you remember how this father would have been dressed. He wouldn't have been wearing pants or jogging shorts but long, cumbersome robes. In that time it was dishonorable for an older man to run, exposing his legs in the process. But this father again demonstrated his love by sacrificing his own dignity in deference to his son. He hiked up his robes and went barreling down the road as fast as he could run.

What kind of father was this?

Can you imagine what his son must have thought when he finally looked up and saw his father bearing down on him? Could he tell if he was joyful or angry? He must have thought the latter, for he launched into his prepared speech even before his father got there. "I am not worthy to be called your son. Make me like one of your hired men."

But his words were not even acknowledged by the father, as he reached his son and swallowed up the words with hugs and kisses of delight. Not a hint of anger came from the father, nor would he talk one moment about the son's offer to be his servant. He was too overcome with joy; the son he'd awaited had found his way home.

Moments later the father's servants arrived. They must have seen him running down the road and chased after him, anxious to see what the father would do to his selfish son. What a shock it must have been for them to come upon such a festival of celebration. The father turned to them. "Get a robe, a ring, and a new pair of sandals. Stoke up the fire and let's get ready to celebrate."

A party? For the son who squandered the family inheritance on his own selfish pleasures? How could this be? The son deserved punishment, not a party!

What kind of father was this?

WHAT THE FATHER WANTED MOST

Isn't it amazing how at each point in the story this father acted completely the opposite of how we would expect a loving father to act?

He should never have given such an irresponsible son an early inheritance. He shouldn't have stood by while his son wasted away. And certainly he shouldn't have welcomed him home so extravagantly without making him pay for his stupidity. The father's actions make no sense at all, unless he wanted something more for his son than mere responsible behavior.

Though it may appear that what the son wanted drove this story, a closer look shows just otherwise. What the father wanted is the key here, and he wanted it so desperately he would spare nothing to have it. What do you think that was?

Was it to be with his sons or to have them labor in his fields? No, the story started there. He could easily have refused his son's request and given him no opportunity to make such a wreck of his life. That wasn't enough for this father. He wanted something more.

What he didn't have was a loving relationship with either of his sons. The younger son saw him only as a conduit to his own pleasures, the elder as a taskmaster to serve in the fields. They were both in the house, but neither was at home in his love. Could that be why the father let the younger son go? Rather than force him to stay and deepen his hostility, the father let him go so he could run to the end of his own self-sufficiency and find out who his father really was.

For it was at that moment, when he looked with longing at the food given to the pigs, that he realized his father was a much kinder man than the farmer he was working for. It was then that he came to his senses and decided to go home. But he still had no idea what kind of father he was about to meet. Afraid of his anger, embarrassed by the mess he'd made of his life, he prepared a speech, confessing his unworthiness to ever again be considered a son.

Even then he had no idea how loved he was, and that nothing he had done in the intervening years had compromised that love.

This father wanted an intimate friendship with both of his children. He wanted them to know how deeply they were loved and to experience their love in return. He didn't want his sons' obedience, but their hearts. Knowing this would happen only when the son truly understood who his father was, he risked it all by letting the son have what he wanted. Only by coming to the end by himself would the son recognize what had been important to the father all along.

As a parent of adult children, I understand that. There's nothing I prize more with my children than those moments when we share the honesty and intimacy of friendship. When they know I love them, and they respond the same way to me, there's nothing better.

That's the point of Jesus' story. The father was not manipulating the son by anything he did. He was only loving the son at the deepest possible level. That love explains why the father let him go in the first place and why he rushed so hard to embrace him. He knew his son's sin had been punishment enough. He ran because he didn't want his son to hurt one second longer than was absolutely necessary. His pain had brought him home. Nothing else mattered.

God feels the same way about you. He's not interested in your service or sacrifice. He only wants you to know how much you are loved, hoping that you will choose to love him in return. Understand that, and everything else about your life will fall into place; miss that, and nothing else will make any difference.

LIVING LESS LOVED

In this incredible story, when do you think the father loved his son the most?

Every time I share this story I ask people that question. Almost always the first answer is the moment where the father met the son on the road. After a bit more thought, however, some suggest it might be when the father gave him his inheritance and let him go. Only then does it become clear: there is no point in the story where the father loves his son more than at any other point. He loved him completely through the whole process. It is the only constant in the story.

The events in this story cannot be accounted for by the varying love of the father—only the varying perception of it by the son. Though he was not less loved at any point in the story, through most of it he lived as if he were.

When he took the money from his father and stormed off the farm, grateful to be out from under his clutches and free to pursue his own way, he lived less loved.

When he spent this money in a foreign land, wasting it on his own pleasures and thinking he'd finally fooled his father, he lived less loved.

Even when he started for home, practicing his plea of repentance, willing to be a slave, he lived less loved.

But finally, when he was home in the robe, the sandals, and the ring, sitting at his father's table, sinking his teeth into the filet mignon, it finally sank in. He was loved. But he always was! It was just that then he could stop living as if he weren't.

Most of our lives are spent living less loved.

When we worry that God will ask us for some horrible sacrifice, we live less loved.

When we indulge ourselves in sin, we live less loved.

When we give in to anxiety in the crush of our circumstances, we live less loved.

When we try to earn God's favor by our own efforts, we live less loved.

Even when we get caught up in religious obligations to make ourselves acceptable to him, we live less loved.

That is the story of the older brother. At the end of the story he was so angry at his father for welcoming his wayward brother home, he refused to come to the house and join the celebration. He had stayed with his father, never pursuing his own aims, but he still missed out on the relationship his father wanted with him. Though a son, he saw himself only as a slave and every request of his father as an onerous chore.

The first son represents those who run from God by indulging their own selfish pursuits; the older son represents those who work hard to impress God with their commitment. Fearful of the consequences of disappointing God, they slave away for him. But they never come to the depth of relationship the Father wants with them. The Pharisees in Jesus' day were like that, as are many people today who are caught up in a host of religious activities but miss out on what it really means to live in the Father's love.

In the long run it doesn't matter whether rebellion or religion keeps you from a vibrant relationship with the Father; the result is still the same. He is cheated out of the relationship he wants with you, and you never come to know how he feels about you.

Jesus ended the story at an interesting point. The younger son was in the house enjoying his newfound relationship with his father. The older son was still outside weighing his options. Would he come to know just how much he was loved and join the celebration, or would he remain convinced of his father's unfairness and stay angry and alone outside?

The choice was his—and it is yours! Everything about your life hinges on the answer to one simple question: Do you know how loved you really are?

Isn't it about time you found out?

> *I pray that you, being rooted and established in love, may have power, together with all the saints, to grasp how wide and long and high and deep is the love of Christ, and to know this love that surpasses knowledge—that you may be filled to the measure of all the fullness of God.*
> —EPHESIANS 3:17–19

For Your Personal Journey

Ask God to show you where you live less loved. What does it make you do: run your own way like the younger brother or work even harder like the older one? God wants you to know that there is nothing you can do to make him love you any more today, and nothing you can do that will make him love you any less. He just loves you. Ask him to teach you how true that is so you can live in freedom.

For Group Discussion

1. Take a moment to share whether or not you identify more with the older son or the younger son and why.

2. What did you learn about God's love in this parable?

3. What kinds of things have you done when you've felt "less loved" by God?

4. Think of some ways that God has demonstrated his love for you, even when you did nothing to earn it.

5

*The great danger facing all of us . . .
is that some day we may wake up
and find that we have been busy
with husks and trappings of life and
have really missed life itself. That is
what one prays one's friends may
be spared—satisfaction with a life
that . . . has in it no tingle or thrill
that comes from a friendship with
the Father.*

PHILLIPS BROOKS (1835–1893), *SERMONS*

Welcome Home

I'VE SEEN THAT LOOK at least a dozen times. *Should I
trust or should I not?*

I know well the battle that rages not fifteen yards from me
as the latest stray puppy tries to decide whether I'm safe or
not. The torment is unbearable. She takes a few halting steps
forward, then thinks better and turns her head away as if to
break a spell about to overcome her. I would love to rush in,
scoop her off her feet, and convince her how safe I am for
her, but if I so much as lean forward, she scurries even farther
into the darkness. Right now, the dog across from me has no
idea what awaits her if she can overcome her fear.

All the benefits of my house are hers if she comes, and they are considerable. The long list of stray or abandoned puppies that have shown up in our front yard makes me wonder if our address isn't scratched on a fire hydrant somewhere because my wife must be the softest touch in town when it comes to a dog without a home.

Here strays receive the royal treatment, complete with a flea bath, loving attention, and plenty of food and water. During the following week my wife will do everything she can to locate the owner. Failing that, she will take an ad out in the newspaper promising a free puppy to a good home and will let it go only when she's convinced the new family will treat her puppy well.

Many warm up to the attention right away, but others act as if they've been beaten by every human they've ever known. Instead of running toward the open gate, the lighted doorway, and all the love they could handle, they shrink back in the shadows, unsure whether it's safe.

The latest puppy is one of those. I hold out my hand, offering her food. I know she hasn't eaten in a while because I can count every rib right through her fur. I coax lovingly, speaking in soft tones, trying to caress her with my words. This won't be easy. I will not force her into my home and allow her fears to be a risk to my children and my dogs. If she comes, she'll have to come willingly.

The game will go on for a while, and right now it could go either way. Will I take care of her and help her, or will I be like all the others who have hurt or abandoned her? She doesn't want any more pain, preferring to leave now if my invitation will only add more grief.

I know exactly how she feels. Every time I play this game, I can't help but think how much this mirrors God's entreaty to me, and the difficult time I have learning to trust him. The choice to trust is never easy—not for stray dogs, nor for stray sons and daughters.

A PLACE PREPARED

In my Father's house are many rooms; if it were not so, I would have told you. I am going there to prepare a place for you. And if I go and prepare a place for you, I will come back and take you to be with me that you also may be where I am.

—JOHN 14:2–3

Could the invitation be any clearer? Jesus told his followers about a house, with a Father who waits for them to come and take their place in his home. Does this sound familiar?

We so easily miss the point of his words when we mistakenly relegate them to the distant future involving a second coming and mansions in heaven. It is more likely that Jesus was still talking about his first going-away—his death on a cross—and his first coming-back—the Resurrection. These events would unfold in the next few days, and Jesus wanted his followers to understand just how important they were.

The cross stands as the pivotal event in opening the door for us to dwell in the Father's love. The apostle Paul told us that when we really understand what happened there between a Father and a Son, we will know for certain and forever just how deep their love is for us. Later on we'll take a look from this vantage point at the power of the cross.

He was going to open a door and return after the Resurrection to show them how to live in his Father's house—the place in the Father's heart he's prepared for each one of them.

The disciples, however, couldn't make sense of his words. When he told them they knew the way to where he was going, Thomas challenged him: "We don't know where you are going, so how can we know the way?"

"I am the way and the truth and the life," Jesus answered.

He knew they were confused. He knew they didn't understand the new relationship they would be able to have with him and his Father after the Resurrection. But he said it simply: "You know me! I will get you there." Notice how he focused not on the process they would have to follow, but on the person they would need to know. He took it right back to relationship again. "Stay with me; you'll know everything you need to know."

A FATHER YOU CAN TRUST

To have the relationship God desires with you, and for which your heart must be crying out or you wouldn't still be reading this book, you simply have to learn to trust him.

I know that is far easier to talk about than it is to do. We've learned all our lives that trusting other people will often leave us frustrated and disappointed. Even the people who love us the most have probably failed us at some point. The lesson our flesh teaches us from a very young age is to take care of ourselves because no one else will.

Perhaps like some of the strays who have come to our house, everyone you've ever trusted has betrayed that trust. Maybe you even feel that God has betrayed your trust when he didn't do things for you that you thought a loving Father would do. If the truth be told, many of us have been exploited by people who came to us in God's name, claiming to know God's will for us, who only wanted to exploit us to meet their own needs.

My heart goes out most of all to those whose earthly fathers betrayed their trust and whose pasts are marred by failure and brokenness. I know some of you keep reading this book because the message stirs you. But every time you read the word "father," something cringes inside you. It's not a term of endearment to you, but one that scratches at old wounds.

For you, "father" only conjures up images of abuse or abandonment. It amazes me that so many who hunger to know God had fathers who were so broken they couldn't even reflect the smallest hint of love to their own children. Either selfishly seeking their own pleasure or using others as a punching bag for their own pain, they left a wake of wounded children who don't know what it is like to have a loving father.

Betrayal by the people we most want to love us can leave deep scars. But even these are not beyond God's ability to heal and redeem. In fact, the reason those wounds hurt so deeply is because God created us to be loved by a Father who puts even the best earthly examples to shame. Even those of us who had good fathers can't imagine how much greater a Father he really is. Even the best fathers, as we saw in the last chapter, can't hold a candle to the love the eternal Father has in his heart for us.

It may take a while, but God can help us define his fatherhood based not on the failed record of broken humanity, but on what it really is to be loved by the most awesome Father in the universe.

So even if the word "father" doesn't convey the most tender image to you, please don't write yourself out of God's house. Learning to trust him is the most difficult thing any of us will ever learn to do. If I can understand that for a stray puppy cowering in my front yard, how much more does the Father of heaven and Earth understand our wounds and our insecurities?

With incredible patience and love, he coaxes us out of our fears to embrace him. He waits for that moment when suddenly we know we are safer in him than in any other place we could be. You may be timid at first, but turn toward him and abandon yourself to trust him in the smallest way you can.

He understands how afraid you are that you'll be disappointed once again. But he's still there, patiently extending his hand to you. He will try to get closer, until you cower away in fear. Then he will back off so as not to add to your pain, hoping his gentleness will one day win you over.

TRUST ONLY HIM

Trust: it is so easy to talk about but so hard to put into practice. Nothing is more theologically certain than that God is faithful and trustworthy. But learning how to live in that trust through the twists and turns of our lives is the most difficult challenge we face.

It took God almost Abraham's entire life to teach Abraham the joy of trusting him. But he did it. Finally when the patriarch was asked to give up his only son and heir, he trusted God's plan and God's nature enough to set about the task. This, from the one who had risked his wife's virtue by lying to Pharaoh and saying that she was not his wife. This, from the one who had impregnated his wife's maidservant when it didn't appear God would give Sarah the child he had promised.

To accomplish that, God did some extraordinary things for Abraham. Rest assured, God knows how difficult it is for you to trust him. He is not threatened by that or angry with you as you struggle in learning to do so.

He simply wants you to keep your eye on him and learn.

He knows that only by trusting him can you participate in relationship with him and enjoy the fullness of life in his household. He also knows you'll trust him only to the degree that you are certain of his love for you.

This is why he created you and why he designed such an extraordinary plan to teach you exactly how to lay aside your fears and walk into his arms. Then he can scoop you up, hold you closely to himself, and fulfill what began in his heart for you before the creation of the world.

This is the journey of a lifetime—to learn to trust him more and more every day for the rest of our lives. The more we trust him, the more of his life we can experience. But don't try to do this on your own. You don't have it in you. He can take you by the hand and teach you just how much you are loved so that you no longer have to pursue your own way and protect yourself in ways that seem only to backfire, hurting you and others around you.

NICE GOD OR MEAN GOD?

We had just completed a spirited discussion on God's grace from Paul's Letter to the Galatians at a men's retreat in the Sierra Nevada mountains. For some time a young man had been waiting until enough people cleared out so we could talk privately.

"Over these two days I've listened to you talk about God as a loving Father. Since I became a Christian I have served only a mean God, fearful every day that I might miss his will and be rejected. I really want to believe he is the incredible Father you speak about, but I've decided not to."

"Really?" I asked. "Why is that?"

"I'm just not sure you're right. I've thought about this over the last day or so, and I've made a decision. I'm going to keep serving the mean God." He had it all worked out. "The way I figure it, if I'm right and serve the mean God, then I'll be fine on Judgment Day. If I'm wrong and he is the Father you're talking about, he will understand why I did what I did.

"If I change now and serve this loving Father, what happens if he turns out to be the mean God I've always thought him to be? Then I'm in trouble."

"Certainly, that's your choice," I told him. "But before you decide, can I ask you a question?"

"What's that?"

"Would the God you're serving ever trade his life on a cross for yours?"

He looked up at me and shook his head emphatically. "No way!"

"Then how can he be the God of the Bible? God knew it wouldn't be easy for us to accept such an incredible offer of friendship, which is why he went to such lengths to convince us."

I was with him only for a weekend and I don't know how he has lived since, but he is like so many others I've met along the journey. Out of the dissonant portraits of God, they have decided that it is safer to treat him as the mean God.

They don't have any idea just how wrong they are.

And they don't know that fearing a demanding God will never be enough to take them into the house. They will never be able to do enough to earn what he wants to give them.

To enter the house, we must trade our fear of him for a love that is far stronger.

> Come to me, all you who are weary and burdened, and I will give you rest. Take my yoke upon you and learn from me, for I am gentle and humble in heart, and you will find rest for your souls.
> —MATTHEW 11:28–29

For Your Personal Journey

What reservations do you have about entrusting yourself completely to God? Realize that the only way to grow in trust is to grow in the knowledge of his love. Ask him every day to reveal the depth of his love to you and in doing so to teach you how to trust him more.

For Group Discussion

1. Have you ever felt like that stray puppy, afraid to trust because of past disappointments?

2. Recall some of the events from Abraham's story (Gen. 12–23) that God used to teach him trust.

3. Share your own stories of how God has taught you to trust him in the past.

4. What are some of the ways we can grow to better know God's love?

What Fear Could Never Achieve

There is no fear in love.
But perfect love drives out fear, because
fear has to do with punishment. The one who fears
is not made perfect in love.

—1 John 4:18

God is good.
You are bad.
Try harder!

<small>THE OBSERVATIONS OF A FIFTEEN-
YEAR-OLD SUMMING UP AN EVENING
WITH HER YOUTH GROUP</small>

The Tyranny of the Favor Line

WHO COULD BLAME the young mother? I certainly couldn't.

She was in her early thirties, the mother of two children. I don't remember the congenital disease her youngest child had, but at six years of age he was already confined to a wheelchair. Often his parents rushed him to the hospital in such critical condition that they were never sure they would bring him home again.

Every time I was with them, I was touched by not only the depth of their need but also the sweetness with which they seemed to endure it. They had grown up in Christian homes and had sought to follow God faithfully into their adult years. I often prayed for them and their child, hoping he would someday be healed.

I had no idea, however, that the stress of his illness was also shredding their marriage. I called them one morning after I had not seen them for a few weeks. I found a devastated mother on the other end of the phone. Her husband had left her two weeks before, and she now had sole responsibility for their sick boy.

Overwhelmed with pain, she told me that she was no longer sure God even existed. If he did, he was not the God she had thought him to be. Not only had six years of praying for her son's healing proved fruitless, but the need had also destroyed her marriage. She was alone, disillusioned, and angry.

I tried to tell her that God still loved her and cared about her needs, but she rebuffed my encouragement. "Do you have any idea what it is like not to be able to ever just relax and enjoy your own child, because you are never sure he will be there tomorrow?"

I told her honestly that I did not. I only had a brief taste of anything similar. Our firstborn daughter had a severe case of jaundice, and I remember how resentful I felt having to take her for a daily blood test and watch my baby scream in pain as they drew it from her toes. That lasted only a week and her life was never in jeopardy. How do you multiply that by six years of standing at death's door with your little boy?

I did offer to help her with whatever resources we had to get her through the days ahead, but she declined. "I just can't keep living this way," she sobbed. "Whatever God expects of me, I just don't have it to give."

Rarely in my life have I felt as inadequate as I did the moment I placed the phone back in its cradle. After nearly fifteen years of pastoral ministry, I didn't have the answers she needed. Only later did I learn why. At the time I was caught in the same trap she was, only on the other side of it. She thought her overwhelming need pointed to her faithlessness and loss of favor with God, while I thought my more pleasant circumstances were proof that I had been faithful and thus had earned his favor.

We both were living under the tyranny of the favor line. She was already paying for it; I was about to.

THE FAVOR LINE

What is the favor line? It's the invisible line that tells us whether or not we've met enough of someone's expectations to merit approval. It's impossible to live in this world without recognizing the favor line's impact on every area of life.

Our parents had one. We knew what made them proud of us, what brought their displeasure or even anger. If your parents' expectations were fair you could play the favor line, acting especially kind when you wanted something from them, or hiding behind their backs what you knew would merit punishment. If your parents' expectations were unreasonable, then maybe you grew up without any approval at all.

We found the same favor line when we went to school, though it existed there in a graduated scale. The higher the expectations we met, the better the grade we received and the greater the approval from teachers and parents.

It didn't take us long to discover that our friends had favor lines as well to derive the benefits of their friendship. Disappoint them, however, and our so-called friends could turn on us in a heartbeat—as we would on them. We found the same line in the work world as well. Those who achieved or exceeded expectations found themselves in the bosses' good graces, with all the perks that favor brought.

We've learned to survive in this world by currying favor where we need it, so it is only natural to assume that God has a favor line as well.

As long as our circumstances are pleasant, or even bearable, we may not think much about God's favor. But let trouble or disappointment encroach on our quiet existence and we begin to wonder how God feels about us. *Does he love me? Have I offended him? Am I doing enough for him to like me?* Struggling with those questions brings us right back to the favor line as we look for some way to get back on God's good side.

King David expressed so eloquently how the favor line superimposes itself on our pursuit of God:

> LORD, *who may dwell in your sanctuary?*
> *Who may live on your holy hill?*
> *He whose walk is blameless*
> *and who does what is righteous,*
> *who speaks the truth from his heart*
> *and has no slander on his tongue.*
> —PSALM 15:1–3

He continued with a list of traits that qualify people to come before the holy God. Other lists in Scripture seem to underline his assertion—the Ten Commandments, the Great Commission, the fruits of the Spirit, just to name a few. It is easy to see why people who seriously pursue God end up with a favor line drawn across their lives and why they think they can assess at any moment how God feels about them by whether they are living above or below it.

Bible reading, prayer, church involvement, and helping others seem to put us above the line. Selfish motives or sinful actions push us beneath it. That would seem easy enough, except that we're never sure how much of any of these things actually matter.

I've asked audiences all over the world this question: "How many of you think that you pray enough? Read the Bible enough? Or witness enough?" I've never gotten so much as one person to raise a hand to my query.

I know what they are thinking because I've thought it, too. *How much is enough, after all? If I pray an hour a day, couldn't I as easily do two? If I read two chapters a day, should I be reading four? Do I need to witness once a month, once a week, to every stranger I meet?*

In the same way, we know in our more genuine moments that we are not entirely free of sin. We may be able to hide it well enough, but thoughts, motives, and hidden deeds all expose our ongoing struggle with sin and doubt. Can we ever be sure how many of our failures God is willing to overlook as part of our maturing process?

That's why I call it the "tyranny of the favor line." Trying to live under the weight of David's list, or anyone else's, would disqualify every one of us from God's presence and his favor. If you've tried it you know how hard it is to do everything you think he requires. The only way to feel good about it is when you think you're at least doing more than other believers around you. But you know intrinsically that you'll never be good enough.

This problem is compounded whenever we encounter difficult or painful circumstances. Who doesn't wonder at such times if he or she is being punished for not being good enough? We joke about it in the most trivial ways, such as getting stopped at consecutive stoplights. "Wow, you must not be living right," someone invariably observes.

But it's no joking matter when we suddenly lose a job or face a life-threatening disease. The tyranny of the favor line is unrelenting, never allowing us to be certain of how God feels about us. So we're left to pick through our circumstances: *He loves me! He loves me not!*

A FAR BETTER PLAN

Is it any wonder, then, that my young friend would sum up the ministry of her youth group by saying, "Same old thing, Dad. God is good. You are bad. Try harder!" Unfortunately, too many people think that's the essence of the gospel and yet on that basis none of us could ever stand before him.

Even David knew that in his more desperate moments. As he hid in a cave from those who sought to kill him, he cried out for God's mercy. "Do not bring your servant into judgment, for no one living is righteous before you" (Ps. 143:2). Aware of his own weaknesses, he was not willing to stake God's favor on his performance.

Later, as David prostrated himself over the public exposure of his adultery and the murder of the cheated husband, and as he grieved the loss of the son his affair produced, he again sought another standard: "The sacrifices of God are a broken spirit; a broken and contrite heart, O God, you will not despise" (Ps. 51:17).

The truth of the matter is, the same Scriptures that give us lists of qualifications to earn God's favor also clearly state that there is not enough goodness in any one of us to fulfill those requirements. Only Jesus would be able to do so. No matter how much we try to earn his favor, we will always fall short. The more effort we give, the more distant he will seem.

Why? Because the favor line causes us to swing between periods of self-pity and self-righteousness. When we recognize our shortcomings, we want to give up in despair. But even when we feel good about our efforts, we cannot understand why God doesn't make himself as real for us as Scripture seems to indicate he is capable of doing. Self-righteousness can be a far greater deterrent to the relationship God wants with us than our failures and mistakes.

When our best-intentioned efforts go unrewarded, we may become disillusioned and drift away. For great periods of time we find ourselves distracted from even thinking about our relationship with God and try to satiate our hunger with a host of other things: our work, other people, religious services, or even buying new things. Though these may work for a while, in quieter moments the hunger returns. None of these things will ever satisfy the hunger that longs to know the living God.

That's why trying to live in service to the favor line will at some point leave you stranded in hopelessness. Either like Peter, after he denied Jesus on the night his friend needed him most, you will be disillusioned by your own failure to do the good you know to do, or like Job you will question whether or not God even loves you or treats you fairly.

God never wanted us to end up in either place. He instead invites us to not walk the tightrope of the favor line but to discover a far better way to know him.

AN INCREDIBLE SURPRISE

At a young age he had already advanced well beyond his peers. Educated in the best schools, he was recognized as one of the most influential religious leaders in one of the best-known cities of the world. His morals and wisdom were impeccable.

But all was not as well on the inside as it appeared on the outside. For all his diligence and wisdom, something ate at him deep within. He was an angry man. He rarely let it show except in acceptable moments of righteous indignation, but in times alone he knew it was there, blackening his soul.

His zeal to be the best servant of God in his generation had not led him to the lap of a loving Father, but to the cruel tyranny of his own ego. He had started out with a desire to serve God, but that passion had quickly been consumed by his desire for spiritual status. He loved the looks of admiration and awe that he saw in the eyes of his friends and mentors.

Then one day, on a journey to a distant city, he came face-to-face with the living God. His encounter was far more dramatic than most. A bright light appeared out of nowhere, knocking him to the ground and blinding his eyes. As he lay there in the dirt, a voice rumbled over his body. "Saul, Saul, why are you persecuting Me?" (NASB).

His next words are quite revealing. "Who are You, Lord?" (NASB).

He knew he was being confronted by the living God. But wait! Didn't the voice say *Saul* had been persecuting *him*? Surely Saul must have wondered in those brief seconds, *Could this be Jesus?*

What if it was? Saul had killed many of his followers and was on his way to kill many more. He regarded them as heretics and sought to crush them and their teaching before they could destroy the faith he had embraced since his youth.

Finally the voice spoke again. "I am Jesus, whom you are persecuting"

His worst fears had been realized. The people he had killed in God's name were in fact God's people. What would come of him now? What punishment awaited him in his blind helplessness? Like a man who closes his eyes, cringing in anticipation of being struck by a raised fist, he slowly realized that no punch was coming. There was no anger, no vengeance.

Saul, later to become Paul the Apostle, had faced the one he had actively warred against, and in that moment all he found was love. The Jesus whom he had persecuted loved him. He had not come to punish Paul but to open his spiritual eyes to see not as he imagined him to be, but as he really was.

In that moment Saul discovered God's favor when he had done absolutely nothing to earn it. Instead of being punished, he received an invitation to come into the family he had tried so hard to destroy. Instead of the death he'd brought to others, he was offered a life that he never knew existed.

Saul was left with one inescapable fact: he had done nothing to propel himself above the favor line but found himself there nonetheless. He found that Jesus had loved him even when he had no idea who he was. For Jesus had shattered the favor line to free Saul from its tyranny. It changed him more than all he'd previously learned about God.

This is where relationship with God begins. It may sound impossible, especially if you've hoped for this in the past and, like the young mother at the beginning of this chapter, you have only been disappointed by how remote he seemed when you needed him the most. All you knew to do was try even harder to be good enough to win his affection.

But such thinking will never lead you closer to him. Instead of teaching you to love him, it will only leave you angry and frustrated that you can't do enough, or that he isn't being fair to you. He wants to break this cycle the only way he can—by making his favor a gift instead of something you earn.

I have long since lost touch with that mother. If I could speak to her today, I'd want her to know that finding favor with God has nothing to do with what we do for him, but what he has already done for us.

> Have mercy on me, O God,
>   according to your unfailing love;
> according to your great compassion
>   blot out my transgressions.
> Wash away all my iniquity
>   and cleanse me from my sin.
>
> —PSALM 51:1–2

<><><><><><><><><><><>

For Your Personal Journey

Have events in your past left you disappointed with God's love for you or overwhelmed you with your own failures? If so, find some time alone with God to go over those moments with him. Ask him to show you how thinking you had to earn his favor might have distorted your perspective of what was really going on. As a regular part of your prayers, ask God to show you where you are trying to earn his favor and ask him to help you see how much he takes delight in you as a loving Father.

For Group Discussion

1. Have you ever felt like the woman with the sick child? How did you resolve those moments in your life?

2. Where do you feel that you walk the tightrope of the favor line in your relationship with God? Where do you feel guilt for not doing enough?

3. Read Saul's conversion story in Acts 9:1–9. Why did Jesus do this for him? What do you think Saul did to qualify for this moment?

4. Pray together that God will teach you how to know him as he really is.

With what shall I come before the LORD and bow down before the exalted God? . . . Shall I offer my firstborn for my transgression, the fruit of my body for the sin of my soul?

MICAH, A PROPHET (C. 700 BC)

What Shall I Give to God?

SOMETIMES YOU JUST CAN'T give things away. At a garage sale my wife and I had before a recent move, I spied a man looking at a reel of electrical wire. We were winding down and I certainly didn't want to throw it away. As he put it down and started to walk away, I told him he could take the wire if he wanted it. He wanted it but wouldn't take it for free. He walked over to hand me a dollar. I refused. He insisted. We compromised and I gave him fifty cents in change.

We often treat God that way, too. When we realize we cannot earn his love, our fallback position is to try to compensate him for it. Particularly when we need him to do something for us we will often find ourselves wondering what we can give to him, or give up for him, that will prove our sincerity.

But what can we give to merit his affection? Is tithing enough? What if he wants everything that I own? Could that be enough? After all, life is more than possessions. Maybe he wants all of my time, too, denying myself any enjoyment or relaxation. Or worse, what if he wants me to go to some far-off land and spend the rest of my life spreading the gospel? How many times has that been promised by those on the brink of death, hoping it would convince God to spare them?

But where does that thinking lead? The prophet Micah took it to its obvious end. Aware of his own sinfulness, he begs this exact question: "With what shall I come before the LORD?

"Shall I come before him with burnt offerings, with calves a year old?" It may have fit the prescriptions of the law, but was it enough to cleanse Micah's soul? Not exactly.

"Will the LORD be pleased with thousands of rams, with ten thousand rivers of oil?" He has seriously upped the ante here, but he still doesn't think it enough as evidenced in his next offer. "Shall I offer my firstborn for my transgression?" Trading with God will always lead you to the unthinkable, as it did Micah. He wonders if offering his firstborn son would be sufficient to atone for his failures and qualify for God's favor. As he so poetically put it, shall I give "the fruit of my body for the sin of my soul?"

In the course of human history it is astounding how many cultures came to that conclusion. When Abraham came into Canaan, human sacrifices to Baal, Molech, and many other Canaanite deities were the order of the day. Elsewhere throughout the world child sacrifice abounded in tribal rituals to seek the favor of their gods. Firstborn sons were tied to altars and virgin daughters were offered to fiery volcanoes. If we try to purge our consciousness of guilt by offering a gift, we will always end up offering that which is most valuable to us.

But even that cannot be enough. Trying to compensate God for his mercy will be as futile as trying to earn it, and it will always leave me guessing whether *he loves me or he loves me not.*

"WHY DIDN'T YOU STOP ME?"

We are long past the days of even considering child sacrifice, but that doesn't mean we don't look for other ways to trade favors with God. Money, time, and energy can be used in our attempts to ingratiate God to accept us or work on our behalf. And these in the extreme can destroy us and others around us as surely as worshiping any idol.

No one modeled what it meant to be a committed member of the congregation I used to pastor better than Janice (not her real name). Whenever we needed someone to cook a meal, fill in for a no-show in our children's ministry, or help by spending time with a hurting woman, she was always the first to volunteer. She never said no.

It became so obvious that we actually made announcements that excluded her: "Would anybody but Janice be willing to help out in the nursery today? The person who was supposed to be there called in sick." We all laughed, then waited for someone else to volunteer.

In return for her service, we showered her with praise. We told her what a gift she was to the body and how special she was to God. We told others, in her hearing, what an example Janice was of every member doing his or her part in ministry. If we just had a hundred Janices our congregation would have transformed the city, or so we thought.

There were signs, of course, to all of us that she stretched herself too thin. We knew of struggles in her family and that responsibilities at home went ignored as she was off helping someone else. But frankly, we needed her because others weren't nearly as willing.

One day it came crashing down like a sand castle in the rising surf. What many thought was the enemy trying to destroy her turned out to be God working to set her free. For Janice's serving hadn't entirely come out of her freedom as a loved child of God. Though she had a God-given passion for children and a heart to serve, somewhere in the process those also became the way for her to earn the acceptance of others, and more important, of God.

I left that congregation and found out later that she did as well when I connected with her family some months later. She told me her story. A significant need in her family had caused her to finally give up doing all the ministry others had come to expect of her. Her marriage broke up and she began to ask the difficult questions about her life in God. People who had been blessed by her service soon distanced themselves from her struggle.

God, however, brought others into her life to help her. He reminded her of simpler times when she had enjoyed the confidence that God loved her and accepted her as his daughter. Somehow all her serving had stolen that simple truth from her. She became like a little girl whose father was too busy for her and she had been driven to find a present big enough to catch his attention again.

No matter how many of those presents she brought, it never seemed to be enough, but for far different reasons than she thought at the time. Fearful that she would never again know Father's love the way she had, she allowed the empty place in her heart to be filled by her busy service and the attention from others it earned her. Rather than encouraging her faithfulness, as we thought we were doing, we were only feeding her insecurity, leading her even further from the relationship with God she desired. That insecurity, along with the needs in her own home, brought her to the brink of personal and emotional bankruptcy.

But the loving Father had never taken his eye off her. He allowed her to come to the end of her efforts so she could find out just how loved she was. The events had been painful, but they had transformed her. Then she looked at me with tears in her eyes and a voice that wasn't angry, simply pleading for some kind of understanding. "You were my pastor. Why didn't you stop me?"

Her words hit me like a punch in the stomach as the attention immediately shifted from her healing to my complicity in her brokenness. She might have driven the car off the road, but I had helped fill it with gasoline. What could I say? I apologized to her without making any excuses. I had failed her, pure and simple.

But the reason I had not stopped her wasn't because I didn't care, it was because I had been on the same course as her, and at the time I hadn't known there was anything wrong with it.

AFTER ALL THIS . . .

Never the server that Janice was or facing the same pressures at home, I didn't end up nearly so broken. But, like her, I had a desire to trade my gifts for my Father's affection, and, like her, I had come to the realization that they were never going to be enough.

My experiences with God began at a very young age. My hunger to know him was piqued by hearing how God involved himself in the lives of ordinary men and women. I also knew at a young age that I was far from sinless and took solace in the God of mercy and forgiveness. I also thought I had to put something forward that would prove to him how serious I was about following him. Looking back, I now know that I was seeking approval from him, by my spiritual passion and willingness to obey him to the best of my ability.

During this time I experienced incredible moments of fellowship with God. I saw him intervene in my life in ways that I knew only he could. I heard his voice speak to the depths of my being and guide me in critical decisions. I mistakenly thought he was rewarding my offerings to him and continued to lay at his feet whatever I could find that I thought would please him.

But inside, I was never certain that he loved and accepted me—my gifts and sacrifice, perhaps, but not me. The more I gave the more it seemed he wanted, and the best I could do at any moment was to break even with him. I never knew that God was simply delighted with me as his child.

- Not after thirty-five years of faithfully engaging the spiritual disciplines in varying mixtures and degrees of intensity.
- Not after twenty years of professional ministry as a local church pastor.

- Not even after traveling at personal cost and risk to help God's people in third-world countries.

At any given moment, I was never sure that God deeply loved me. If you had asked me, I would have told you he loved me, and for the most part I believed that to be true. After all, Scripture clearly presses that point and I am comfortable talking in such terms. But that still didn't answer my deeper concern. How did he feel about me on any given day?

HE DELIGHTS IN YOU

The words of the Old Testament prophet seemed only a distant dream, "He will take great delight in you, he will quiet you with his love, he will rejoice over you with singing." Except for fleeting moments, few and far between, I couldn't imagine that this was the way God felt about me. How could he, with the temptations that I battled?

I don't think it takes long for any of us who probe such questions honestly to see enough failures and wasted time to give God ample justification to set us aside and ignore the requests we make of him.

Jesus warned us that there would be people who would prophesy, cast out demons, and work many miracles in his name, whom he would turn away at the Judgment. "I never knew you. Away from me." If that isn't a great example of climbing the ladder that's leaning on the wrong wall, I don't know what is. I didn't want to be caught with that crowd.

These moments of insecurity would drive me to my knees in repentance and make me redouble my efforts to be more committed to God. Though I could sustain the increased burden for a few weeks or months, I never had any certainty that the things I was doing were enough to cause him to be delighted with me. Eventually I would slide back to where I had been before.

I'll never forget when all of that changed. A few years ago, through a painful betrayal and a fresh insight into God's work for us on the cross, I began to see how much my Father loved me and to understand how much delight he took in his children. This realization radically transformed my life, and it is my hope that the telling of it in the pages ahead will help transform yours as well.

God doesn't need us to serve him as a means to attain his love or affection. He wants us to serve him out of the love and affection he already holds for us in his heart. If you have never tasted that reality, you cannot imagine the freedom that lies ahead of you. My Father brought me to the place where I realized that even if I never preached another sermon, never counseled another person, never led someone to Christ again, he would still delight in me as his child.

That doesn't mean he approves of everything I do, but he has freed me to know that he loves me—absolutely and completely. I had served God for thirty-four years, always with an undercurrent of trying to earn his favor. It has only been in the last twelve that I've learned to live in that favor, and I'm never going back.

That's when it became clear. It is not the fear of losing God's favor that takes us to the depth of fellowship with him and transforms our lives with his holiness. It is our certainty of knowing his unrelenting love for us, even in the midst of our weakness and failure, that leads us to the fullness of his life.

Fear had never taken me to the depths of his life or his transforming power; discovering his delight has. I now know that the key to God's favor doesn't rest on what I give him but on what he already has given me.

He delights in you, too. Can you see him that way, exalting and dancing with joy over you?

No? Do you think your failures and doubts diminish his love for you? Are you afraid you can't offer him enough to make him notice you?

Then come with me and let me show you something. He doesn't delight in you because of your deeds or your gifts. He delights in you simply because you are his.

> *The LORD your God is with you. . . .*
> *He will take great delight in you,*

he will quiet you with his love,
  he will rejoice over you with singing.

—ZEPHANIAH 3:17

For Your Personal Journey

Take an honest look at the spiritual things to which you give your life. Are they rising out of your security in God's great love for you or an attempt to earn his affection? Do you live trying to pay God back for his salvation, or some other act of his on your behalf? Ask God to begin to rearrange your thinking and to help you understand that his love goes far beyond any gift you can bring him.

For Group Discussion

1. What kinds of gifts and offerings do people use today to try to earn God's affection?

2. Have you ever gone through a season the way Janice did, working harder but feeling emptier spiritually? What can you learn from that experience?

3. Was there a time in your life when you sensed Father was delighted with you? Was that because you had done something big for him, or because you knew that he loved you just the way you were?

4. Pray together that God will teach you how to find your acceptance in his love alone and not in anything you can do for him or give to him.

*When we accept
ownership of our
powerlessness and
helplessness, when
we acknowledge that
we are paupers at the
door of God's mercy,
then God can make
something beautiful
out of us.*

BRENNAN MANNING, *THE
RAGAMUFFIN GOSPEL*

The Businessman and the Beggar

IT TURNED OUT TO BE a tale of two men. These were
the only two encounters Mark thought significant to record
from Jesus' last trip to Jerusalem and his impending death.
One was at the beginning of the journey, near his home
base of Galilee. The other came on the trip's last leg, in the
city of Jericho before Jesus would travel to Jerusalem.

Two men, each in dire need, approached Jesus for help.
Clearly, Jesus extended his favor to both of them, but as
we shall see, only one received it. The other retreated from
his moment with Jesus, his countenance shattered, grieved
because he had misunderstood the offer Jesus made to him.

Watch each of them carefully. Why did one receive and the
other did not? If you're like me, you'll see yourself in both

of them at various times in your life. But now you'll know which example shows how you respond to God, and which takes your best intentions and turns them against you.

The answer may surprise you because it is the opposite of the ways most of us have been trained to think about God and how he works in us.

CAUGHT IN THE DOING

Jesus had no more begun his journey to Jerusalem than a man ran up to him, stopped him, and knelt before him in the dirt. "Good teacher, . . . what must I do to inherit eternal life?" Both his pace and his posture testified to the desperation in his request. He knew Jesus had something he lacked and wanted to find out his secret before he left town.

The question certainly sounds genuine enough, even humble. Jesus answered by referring him to the commandments.

The businessman's answer tells us a lot about him: "I have kept these things from my youth up" (NASB).

Really? Of course we know now and Jesus knew at the time that this answer wasn't possible. Paul told us that no one has ever kept all of God's Law and that if even one person could have earned eternal life by the Law, then Christ would have died in vain. If this man had been genuine, he would have known that. God had given the Law so that he would come to the end of himself and know he needed someone to rescue him.

Does that mean he was lying? Not necessarily. Though he had not kept the Law, what was most critical in this exchange was that he genuinely thought he had. Since he was a little child he had worked hard to obey the Law in hopes of earning his place in God's kingdom.

For him to think he had kept the Law, however, he had to re-create it in his own image. In other words, he would have created loopholes in his mind to justify those portions he had not kept, perhaps focusing only on major parts of the Law such as murder and adultery and excusing his own hate, lust, or selfishness.

By his own desperation we know he missed the point. The fact that he was still seeking eternal life made it clear that he hadn't found it yet, nor was he confident that his current course would produce it. He wanted something more to do.

This man was steeped in his own works. That was evident by the question he asked at the outset. The "I" and the "do" gave him away: "What must I do . . . ?" He was focused on himself, his ability and resources, trying so hard to earn what Jesus wanted to give him.

How Jesus wanted him to understand that! Mark specifically mentions that Jesus looked on him with deep affection. What did he see? Did he see a little boy trying to be perfect as the only way to earn his father's affirmation? Did he see the years of fruitless labor this man had endured? Could he see the twisted motives he used to justify himself and maintain his illusion of righteousness? Did he see the gnawing in the young man's stomach, born of his obsessive drive to perfection that was destroying him from within?

Probably Jesus saw all that and more, and he wanted the businessman to see it, too. On the surface, his next response seems to be one of Jesus' most insensitive comments: "One thing you lack: go and sell all you possess and give to the poor, and you will have treasure in heaven; and come, follow Me" (NASB). On hearing the words, the businessman's countenance fell. Unable to do that, he walked away in grief.

How often I've taught this parable and, with unwitting arrogance, railed at the rich man's inability to do what Jesus asked of him. He was too greedy to follow Jesus, I said. He loved his money more than God and now he would pay for it.

But honestly, was that Jesus' point? Who would have come to this kingdom if those were the terms? When I first went forward at a Billy Graham crusade, all I was asked to do was repent and believe in him. If he'd asked me to sell everything I owned and give it to the poor, I doubt I would have gone forward. I doubt anyone else would have either. In fact, I've never met one person who ever came to Christ on those terms nor many who would stay if he required it of them today!

To condemn the man for not doing so is not only arrogant of us but misses Jesus' point entirely. He was not offering the man the opportunity to buy his salvation. He only wanted him to discover what his attempts to keep the Law already should have—that he didn't have enough in himself to meet any standard of qualification for God's life.

RAISING THE BAR

Coaches don't train young high jumpers by putting the bar at world-record height and challenging them to jump it. They put it at a height their charges can successfully achieve and then, over the course of time, slowly raise the bar to allow refined technique, practice, and conditioning to help them jump higher.

But Jesus didn't do that here. Responding to the rich man's request, Jesus put the bar forty feet in the air. *Jump that!* And the rich businessman did exactly what any athlete would do: he went away discouraged, knowing the task was impossible.

The man understood the lesson but missed the point. Jesus wasn't trying to be mean to him. He raised the bar beyond the man's ability to get over it precisely because Jesus wanted him to stop trying. The gift he offered the man was to be free of the incredible burden of having to earn God's love by his own efforts. He was caught in his own doing and Jesus was trying to free him.

He was hoping the young man would look him in the eye and say, "I can't do that!" To which Jesus might have answered, "Good, then stop doing all the other silly things you're trying to do to earn God's favor. Stop striving, stop pretending, stop trying to earn that which you can never earn!"

Jesus didn't want him living any longer under the tyranny of the favor line, but he knew how difficult it is for people of great resources to find their way into his kingdom. Such people tend to feel they can earn it or pay for it. They are too focused on their own efforts and resources to receive the simple beauty of God's gift.

The businessman's dependence on his own resources was robbing him of the life he sought. No matter how much he could do, such efforts would never cover the empty place in his heart that sought God's approval. For only in realization can we discover what it really means to be approved as God's children and find security in his love for us.

That's not to say that as we love him he won't bring us greater freedom from our possessions and show us the joy of generosity, for he will. But that will rise not out of our attempts to earn his favor, but as grateful responses to the favor he already offers us.

Even when Peter started to boast that he and the others had left everything to follow him, Jesus reminded him that none of them had left anything that he wouldn't replace with far more and far better. The fact was, they had left their stuff not to earn eternal life, but because of a relationship with Jesus that had captured their hearts.

Sadly, we don't get to see the end for this young businessman. My hope is that Jesus' words finally worked through his heart. But whether they did or didn't, Jesus still offered him an incredible gift—the secret to God's favor.

"LORD, HAVE MERCY!"

As Jesus was departing Jericho a few days later for his final walk up the barren heights to the city of Jerusalem, another man wanted his help. This man was a blind beggar sitting by the side of the road. He heard a great commotion around him; he wanted to know what it was. Someone told him that Jesus of Nazareth was passing through on his way to Jerusalem for the feast.

Bartimaeus had already heard enough about this teacher from Galilee to know that he had the power to help him. He began to cry out, "Jesus, Son of David, have mercy on me!"

People nearby were embarrassed by his shouts and sternly told him to keep quiet. After all, he was only a beggar. Why would Jesus care about him? But that only made Bartimaeus cry even louder, and above all the other noise Jesus heard him. He had Bartimaeus brought to him and he made his request: "I want to regain my sight!" (NASB).

Notice that he did not ask what he needed to do to see

again. He did not barter based on any qualification he might have had to make him worthy. He simply put all of his confidence in the mercy of the man from God.

And that was enough.

Jesus didn't ask him to sell all he had. Jesus healed him and noted that Bartimaeus's simple focus was all that was needed. "Go; your faith has made you well." (NASB) Not only did he receive healing, but salvation as well.

Jesus did not love the beggar more than the businessman, nor did he give to one and not the other. For he graciously gave to both of them. It's just that one recognized it and one did not; the difference between the two contains all we need to know to find life in God.

Jesus didn't want the disciples to miss that point. Even before he left on this journey he told them a parable that these encounters illustrated perfectly. He told of a Pharisee and a tax collector entering the temple. The Pharisee delighted in his righteousness—how he was more committed than anyone else he knew. He even puffed himself up at the expense of the tax collector praying nearby, saying, "God, I thank you that I am not like other men . . . even like this tax collector."

That's what living by our own, works produces. Since we'll never be good enough on our own, we will seek to justify ourselves by being better than most other believers around us. To create that facade, we have to focus on their weaknesses and hold them in contempt. Anytime we set ourselves above others, we only demonstrate how little we understand God's mercy.

The tax collector, on the other hand, was not even willing to look up to heaven but beat his chest, praying, "God, be merciful to me, the sinner!" (NASB). Then Jesus asked which man went home justified. The answer was obvious, as obvious as Jesus' encounter with the businessman and the beggar.

When you are tempted to stake your relationship with God on your own goodness or your sacrifice, don't even try. Picture the bar so high that you'll never find a way to clear it. Approach God on the basis of your own efforts, and you will always go away disappointed and disillusioned. But that is not bad news.

What it means is that God has fulfilled in himself everything he would ever require of us. Abandoning our own attempts to establish our own worthiness is central to the power of the gospel. Learn that, and a door stands before you that will lead you to the very heart of a loving Father. This is the way to know that he delights over you with joy and is able to transform you into the fullness of his glory.

He absolutely, completely loves you. Discovering how much will revolutionize your relationship with him and your life in this world.

> *Go and learn what this means: "I desire mercy, not sacrifice." For I have not come to call the righteous, but sinners.*
>
> —MATTHEW 9:13

For Your Personal Journey

Spend some time with God considering your own relationship with him. Do your requests of God look more like those of the businessman or the beggar? Do you begin every day aware of your performance or the lack thereof, or is your awareness focused on God's mercy and his affection for you? We've all been taught that life in God is something we earn with diligent effort, and this isn't easy to unlearn. Ask him to help you understand his mercy and how you can stop trying to jump over a bar you will never reach.

For Group Discussion

1. Are you more like the businessman or the beggar in this chapter? Explain why.

2. Describe the bars you've tried to jump over to merit God's favor.

3. Why do you think we have been given so many bars to jump over as proof that we are serious about God's life?

4. What would life be like if you could trust God's mercy for you every day?

5. Pray for one another that you'll learn the difference between mercy and performance.

9

*The Christian
ideal has not
been tried and
found wanting.
It has been found
difficult and left
untried.*

G. K. CHESTERTON

The God We Love to Fear

IT WAS A STRANGE GAME we played as little children. We used to scare ourselves half to death just for the sheer joy of it.

We would be sitting around the front yard of someone's home, when suddenly one of us would point down the street saying we saw a kidnapper sneaking up toward us. The rest of us would mockingly feign to be afraid.

"I'm not kidding," he would say. "I know I saw him looking this way." For a while he would continue the ploy and we would not believe him. Eventually someone else would join the story and point out something he thought looked suspicious, a glance our direction by someone walking up the street, or a car passing by too slowly. Then the game was on.

Everyone contributed to the story in hopes of scaring the

others off the porch. The last one to run was the winner. But we were young and it usually didn't take long. At some point in the process reality would get distorted and we'd all believe our own stories. Suddenly we'd burst off the porch, running for the backyard and down into the safety of the basement.

After a while our fears would subside and, laughing, we would retell how scared we got. Then we'd go out front to see if we could spot any more kidnappers. The whole process would repeat itself until we again ran to the basement for safety.

It was only a game, but it allowed us to taste the power of fear. Even when we were making it up ourselves and dared to resist it, it could still win us over.

A POWERFUL FORCE

If you've ever tried to go to sleep at night with fear preying on your mind, you also know its incredible power. Even when we can rationally discount it, fear nevertheless forces its will upon us, like a relentless rising tide.

Those who motivate people know that nothing works better. I see it in my work helping public schools navigate the treacherous waters where church and state issues collide. All of the letters sent out by advocacy groups on the right and the left appeal exclusively to fear of what the other side is doing to destroy "the America we all hold dear." They know nothing works better to make people send in their money or volunteer their time and energy.

Fear permeates life in this age. It's what makes you go to work in the morning and lock your doors at night, and it makes your heart race when a policeman pulls up behind you. Advertisers use it, and so do friends and family when they want you to do what they think is best.

> And there is so much to fear—
> We fear the unknown.
> We fear being unknown.
> We fear not having enough.

We fear getting caught.
We fear we'll never find the right person to marry.
We fear debilitating or life-threatening diseases.
We fear for our children's safety.
We fear what other people think of us.
We fear they won't.
We fear crime.
We fear losing a loved one.
We fear authority.
We fear that we won't get the things we desire most.
We fear what others might do to us.
We fear rejection.
We fear failure.
We fear being taken advantage of.
We fear being alone.
We fear losing our jobs.
We fear people finding out we're not all we claim to be.
We fear something bad might happen to us.
We fear not fitting in.
We fear death.

No wonder it's not easy to sleep some nights and no wonder we are bombarded with the symptoms of stress, all the way from headaches to depression. Fear is so powerful that almost all of our human institutions use various forms of it to keep people under control. Offering the right combination of rewards and punishments easily exploits people's fears to make them do what they otherwise wouldn't choose to do.

It would be easier to make the point here if fear always led us to do harmful and destructive things, but that simply isn't true. Sometimes fear will lead us to prudent decisions. The fear of getting caught might win over our temptation to do something wrong. The fear of losing our jobs will induce us to work harder than we might otherwise.

In a fallen world, fear is the only way to hold society in check. Caring for nothing more than our own self-interests, the fear of hurtful consequences is the foundation of all laws and authority. Before Jesus died on the cross, there was nothing else. Even God used fear to help keep sin in check among his people. "The fear of the LORD is the beginning of wisdom," wrote the psalmist. We come to the regrettable conclusion that fear isn't our problem—only what we fear. If we can fear the awesome, holy God more than anything else in our lives it will lead us to the right path, or so we think.

Thus we come to view fear in ambivalent terms. Fear of what others might think can lead us down a wrong path, but fearing God can help motivate us to holiness. So we don't end up seeing fear as the problem it is, as long as it is God we fear most.

WON BY FEAR

Just look at the history of Christianity. Teaching people to fear God and his judgments has been used more than any other motive to hold the faithful in check. It is readily accepted now as the best way to get people to follow God.

Saint Cecile Cathedral sits high above every other building in the village of Albi, located in the southern region of France. Like the Sistine Chapel in the Vatican, the ceiling and walls of the magnificent edifice are painted with biblical scenes.

The entire story of the Bible has been painted across the ceiling over a brilliant blue background, beginning at the back of the cathedral with Creation and Eden and finishing in front with the Last Judgment. There, behind the altar and overwhelming it by its sheer size, is one of the largest full-color pictorial compositions in the world, nearly forty feet tall and thirty feet wide. In its original form, the painting depicted God enthroned at the center, judging between the sheep and the goats.

The goats are cast into the torment of hell, agonizingly represented in seven individual panels that take up the entire bottom of the composition. The panels, each fifteen feet in height, show how those guilty of the seven mortal sins will be tormented in hell. For instance, the greedy are shown bound, with demons pouring molten gold down their throats.

Constructed in the fourteenth century, this scene depicts

what the designers firmly wanted in the minds of the faithful as they gathered in the cathedral. God is a terrible judge, and terrible things will happen to those who do not do what he says. It's a refrain often heard in Christian history—even to the present.

Waiting to get into a concert with my wife, we were confronted with a gaggle of signs announcing our imminent consignment to hell. "Don't you care that you are headed for hell?" someone shouted in my face from only a few steps away. "Repent, or you will burn in agony forever!" someone else called out across the crowd.

I've no doubt these people were well-intentioned, seeing this as the best way to lead people to God. It was obvious, however, that the crowd around them was not convinced. Most ignored them, resenting the imposition of their message on a captive audience.

Through most of its history, Christianity has been inseparable from the God of judgment. The panels in the cathedral at Alibi, Jonathan Edwards's "Sinners in the Hands of an Angry God," or the invitation to receive Christ "because you could die tonight and go to hell," all seek to build on this foundation of fear. While it is effective to prompt people to make on-the-spot commitments to Christ, doing so has rarely led to spiritual passion and growth.

Isn't it odd that the most compelling argument in our day to know God is the horror of not doing so? I find no such preoccupation in the ministry of Jesus for those who followed him. Certainly he and writers of the New Testament warned us about the destructiveness of sin and the consequences that befall those who neglect his offer of salvation. But he did not use that fear to induce people to follow him.

He invited those around him to a God who loved them completely and to a kingdom more valuable than anything they had ever known. He didn't use their fears because he knew that fear was part of the problem, even their fear of God. Though it might be easily manipulated to secure a temporal response, it would never be enough to bring them to the fullness of his Father's glory.

WHEN FEAR IS NOT ENOUGH

I thought I'd missed the Rapture, and for a twelve-year-old boy, that can be pretty unnerving.

Through a tragic comedy of errors at my junior high school, I had not received a message my parents had sent telling me not to get on the bus after school. They would be picking me up.

So I boarded the bus as usual. Only this day was different. To start with, my older brothers who always boarded first at the high school weren't there. A few minutes later when we arrived at the grammar school on the route, my youngest brother wasn't in line either. How could this be?

Immediately I remembered the words the pastor had spoken the Sunday before at church. Talking about the second coming of Christ, he told about two people in a field. One was taken, the other left to face the torment of the Great Tribulation. "If there is one unconfessed sin between you and God when Jesus comes again, you'll be left." It didn't take me long sitting on that bus without the rest of my family to come up with a whole list of sins that would have denied my participation in the Rapture.

That bus ride home was the longest of my life. By the time I got to my stop, my imagination had run wild. I was certain now that I had missed the Rapture. I ran up our quarter-mile-long driveway, hoping against hope that at least one of my parents would still be home. They weren't.

I was devastated. I prayed. I cried. I repented. I begged God to take me even if a bit late, but all to no avail. Terrified of the Tribulation to come, I knew that going to hell would be even worse. I then and there determined that I would be faithful to God no matter what the Antichrist tried to do to me. Even though I'd blown the first chance, I would not blow the second. In the arrogance of youth, I prepared myself to face the Antichrist.

An hour later my parents returned with the rest of the family and the miscommunication unraveled. I hadn't missed the Rapture after all! I was elated with the news, but I was taking no chances on the future. I was going to be the best twelve-year-old God ever wanted.

For the next month, I probably was. As best I knew at

the time, I lived sinlessly, avoiding any temptation that surfaced and spending time in prayer and Bible reading every day. But it didn't last. As the days passed, so did the reality of my fear, until some months later I ended up right back where I had begun.

Jesus knew that fear, like a crutch for someone with a broken leg, is only a temporary fix. Though it can be a heady motivation in the short-term, it is absolutely worthless for the long haul. As such it doesn't really change us; it controls us only as long as our fear can be stoked. That's why sermons on God's judgment are so common in Christianity. They confront us with our fears of God and seek to provoke us to live the way we know we should. The repentance that follows and the resolve to rededicate ourselves to Christ's purpose make us feel clean again.

Such experience actually helps us live better for a while—but only for a while. Eventually the passion of such moments fades and the old self encroaches its way back into our lives. We end up caught in the same patterns from which we had repented. Soon the cycle repeats itself.

Fear cannot lead us to lifelong transformation, but to only a momentary reformation of behavior. Instead of inviting us to enter into relationship with the living God, it pushes us away with feelings of inadequacy and repetitious failure.

Jesus had a far better way. He wanted to break the bondage of fear itself—even our fear of God. He knew of a force far more powerful—one that would not fade with the passing of time and would invite us into the depths of relationship with God. He would settle for nothing else. Why should we?

> *Do not be afraid, little flock, for your Father has been pleased to give you the kingdom.*
>
> —LUKE 12:32

<><><><><><><><><><><>

For Your Personal Journey

Think back to the time you first made a commitment to Christ. Did it come because you were overwhelmed with his love, or because you were afraid of his punishment? When you think now of God watching you every moment of every day, do you find that comforting or scary? Do you see fearing him as a necessary motive to help you avoid sin and do the things you think God wants you to do, and if so, has that thinking helped you avoid all the sins in your life? Think through these questions as you ask God to show you how your fear of him might be keeping you from feeling safe in his presence.

For Group Discussion

1. Of the list of fears presented in this chapter, which ones do you normally think are helpful to you? Which ones are harmful? Which ones do you battle the most in your daily life?

2. Has your fear of the Lord helped you avoid harmful actions in your life?

3. Has it been enough to make you stop sinning completely?

4. Tell about a time when the fear of the Lord was very real to you. How did that fear affect your relationship with him?

5. Respond together to what you've shared in prayer, asking God to free you from the slavery of fear.

10

*Won't the awareness
God loves us no matter
what lead to spiritual
laziness and moral
laxity? Theoretically,
this seems a reasonable
fear, but in reality the
opposite is true. . . . The
more rooted we are in
the love of God, the
more generously we
will live our faith.*

BRENNAN MANNING,
LION AND LAMB

The Most Powerful Force in the Universe

"DO YOU LOVE ME?" Is there a harder question you can be asked by someone you care about? It implies that you've done something to suggest otherwise. How do you answer with words when your actions fall so far short?

"Do you love me?" The words must have sliced to the depths of Peter's heart as Jesus probed him. It had been a little more than a week since Peter had abandoned Jesus at his greatest moment of need. After promising he would die for Jesus, Peter's fears had caught up to him. In the heat of the moment, he proved to all that he loved his own life more than he loved his friend.

Jesus had already asked the question twice, referring to

the greatest depth of love any person could offer another. Both times, Peter could not say that he did. In the verbal dance they engaged in that morning on the shore of Galilee, Peter had answered with a different word for "love" than Jesus had used. "I have great affection for you, as a brother," he responded.

We are not told why he couldn't answer with the word that Jesus used, but it is easy to assume his failure might well have played into it. Peter knew he had not loved him as much as he thought, and perhaps in the face of his denial tried to find a word that would more honestly fit his actions.

When he asked him the third time, Jesus switched to Peter's word for brotherly affection. Though Peter answered in the affirmative, he was hurt by the fact that he'd been asked three times. But notice how undeterred Jesus was by his answers. All three times he invited Peter past his weakness to ministry in his kingdom. "Take care of my sheep." His message was clear: "You're not damaged goods. Your failure has not changed anything between us. You're still in the family."

This exchange is fascinating for a number of reasons, but perhaps the most incredible is not the answer he sought from Peter, but the simple fact that Jesus asked the question at all. What God ever cares about being loved?

THE GOD WHO WANTS TO BE LOVED

"Do you love me?"

It's not exactly a question we expect God to ask, and yet John recorded it as one of the significant conversations the resurrected Jesus had with one of his disciples. That he asked it more than once focused even more attention to it.

Why would he care about being loved? He is almighty God, enthroned in the presence of thousands of adoring angels. He can command obedience simply because he is the greatest power in the universe. Why would he be seeking Peter's love?

We seem to be far more comfortable when our deities command fear. Almost every idol or false god man has ever created seeks the submission of his or her subjects by sheer terror. But love? What false god ever wanted to be loved? Feared? Yes! Obeyed? Yes. But never loved.

After his work on the cross was finished, however, Jesus went looking for love, and he sought it from the one who had just failed him most. Could this be what he most wanted the cross to produce in his followers? Was his death designed to reach past their fears of God and begin a new relationship based on the intimacy of love instead? What else could it be?

Throughout the Old Testament, God often identified himself as the God of love and mercy, but few understood him that way. They seemed able to obey him only under threat or judgment. Even commanding them to love him with all their hearts seemed to negate the end by the means employed. Can true love really be commanded?

What Jesus sought from Peter reflected what the Father had always wanted from his people, but what they have rarely understood. He desired the warmth and tenderness of a relationship filled with love. None of this was lost on Peter, even though his answer didn't come easily. If the power of the cross could reach past that failure, then something new had really happened. Jesus was inviting Peter past his failure to experience the depths of God's love—to tap into the most powerful force in the universe.

Love lies at the very core of God's nature. In fact, when John summed up the substance of God, he did so in a very simple statement: "God is love." We may not be able to explain in concrete terms all that God is and how Father, Son, and Spirit relate together in such unity, but we do know that they exist in a perfect state of love.

When that love touches you, you will discover there is nothing more powerful in the entire universe. It is more powerful than your failures, your sins, your disappointments, your dreams, and even your fears. God knows that when you tap the depths of his love, your life will forever be changed. Nothing can prevail over it; and nothing else will lead you to taste of his kind of holiness.

STRONGER THAN FEAR

I am not saying that the fear of God is wrong, only that it is incomplete. It is the first rung on the ladder to knowing God in his fullness. He said himself it was the beginning of wisdom, but it is only the beginning. Love is the end product of wisdom.

If you don't love God, you would be well-served to fear him. At least that might keep you from behaviors that will destroy you and others around you. But once you know how much he loves you, you'll never need to fear him again. In other words, this Father doesn't just seek your obedience, he desires your affection. He can have your obedience without your love, but he knows where he has your love he will also have your obedience.

"There is no fear in love . . . because fear has to do with punishment," John wrote as he tried to convince the church in Ephesus that God's love had replaced the old order of fear. It was revolutionary then and regrettably still is today. We seem more comfortable fearing God than we do loving him.

But fear isn't in God's nature. He fears nothing. Thus his own holiness is produced not by his fear, but by his love. In fact, fear cannot produce the holiness God wants to share with us. It is incapable of doing so. For God to transform us to be like him, he must expel our fear and teach us the wonder of living in his love.

John paints fear and love as polar opposites. Before the coming of Jesus, God used fear to hold our passions in check, but it never made anyone holy. In Christ, God wanted to win our affection with his own. Thus he needs our fear no longer, knowing we will never love that which we fear.

You might honestly believe the highway patrol officer behind you in traffic is looking out for your safety, but that doesn't endear you to him. In fact, the fear of getting a ticket will make you extra careful about every move you make. For the time he is near you in traffic, you are safer than at any other time on the road. Not only are you driving more safely, but so are the other drivers around you.

But does that keep you from being relieved when he finally turns to go another direction? Even though his presence was more helpful to you than you might realize, it didn't make you want to become his friend. The motives of conformity do not produce intimacy.

This is where organized religion so often gets it backward, and why so many people in the pews remain so distant from God and so unchanged in their character. We think conformity to God's ways will lead us closer to him, when the opposite is true. If we focus on our own fears and performance, he will seem more distant. It is only by living in the security of God's affection that he is able to transform us.

Fearing God can compel us to conform our behavior to his desires, but it will not last. Because it convinces us to act against our will, even when it leads us to righteousness, it does not change us. The behavior that results lasts only as long as the fear itself, which is why those who approach it this way will need greater levels of fear to stay motivated.

God knows that responding to his love will take you much further than fear ever could. That's why love must first deal with your fears. "Perfect love drives out fear," John continued. While fear may be the most powerful motive known to man, God's love is more powerful still, and in the face of it our greatest fears are swallowed up in him. Love displaces fear the same way light displaces darkness.

There is nothing more critical to spiritual growth than making this transition. John concludes, "The one who fears is not made perfect in love" (1 John 4:18). As long as we live in fear, we exclude ourselves from the very process that will make us complete in God.

People who serve God because they fear his punishment will forever try to please him by doing the best they can, and they will always come up short. Dominated by guilt and having to justify themselves in failure, they will never discover what it really means to become God's friend.

God has better things in mind for you. He wants you to know his love so completely that fearing him will have no place in your life. When you are absolutely convinced how much God loves you, that knowledge will drive out every fear you have. You won't need to fear an uncertain future, the rejection of friends, the lack of desires, or even God himself. Knowing his heart for you will free you to trust him more than ever, and that alone will lead you to ever-greater participation in his holiness.

WHAT MANNER OF LOVE

You would think being free from the fear of the Lord would be great news, but I don't find that everyone shares my excitement. Many see their fear of God, or eternal judgment, as the only thing that keeps them from indulging in sin. Without it, they are so afraid they might give in to their flesh, they cling to their fear of God as if it were a life raft in a frothing sea.

It is difficult to give up our fear of God if it has served us so well. That's understandable. We don't often think of love as a compelling enough motive to hold us in check. We all know that we loved our parents, but not enough to keep us from doing things they told us not to do. Only the fear of getting caught and punished was enough to deter us from wrongdoing. Many of us transfer that same idea to God, so it is no wonder we trust our fear more than his love.

But the love God extends to us and invites from us is nothing like any love we have known before. "This is how we know what love is: Jesus Christ laid down his life for us" (1 John 3:16). John defines our Father's love for us because he knew that our earthly references to love would never do justice to God's.

Love in earthly terms is invariably tied to self-interest. That's why people talk about falling in love or out of love. What they mean is that they feel affection for someone when that person brings some benefit to them. However, when the person no longer provides benefit, or becomes more of a burden than a joy, they don't feel the same way about them. Haven't we all had what we thought were close friends who turned on us the minute we no longer served their interests? Haven't we done the same to others? Self-centered "love" can seek only its own good.

Only in the rarest moments will someone's love for another call him to deny his self-interest and sacrifice himself for another. Probably the greatest stories in literature play to this theme and are the ones that touch us so deeply.

They provide a glimpse into the eternal. Rare indeed are the relationships in this world that rise to such self-sacrifice.

But that's exactly what Jesus did for us. By doing so he turned the definition of love upside down. God's love is not based on *selfishness*, but *selflessness*. He didn't give his life on the cross to serve himself, but to serve those lost in sin. By doing so he modeled a love for us that we can find only in him. This love gives up its own desires in the face of greater good. It is meant to be not only the subject of fiction, but the way we live every day.

That may seem incredibly remote from your life. We're not wired to think in such terms, having learned from a very young age that if we're going to survive in this world, we have to look out for ourselves. We have no idea how to love selflessly and no ability to conjure up love out of our own commitment or devotion.

John said it best. "We love because he first loved us" (1 John 4:19). Until we experience the reality of God's love and grow to trust him with the details of our lives, we will not break free from the power of self. That's why it is so critical to understand Jesus' death on the cross as an act of love for you. This teaching has been too long neglected among God's family. If you see it only as God satisfying his justice, then you unwittingly empty the cross of its power.

The doorway into the Father's love begins at the cross. Seeing what Father and Son accomplished together in that climactic moment defines love in a way that you can experience only in him. This is the love that will allow you to feel perfectly safe in the Father's presence. It frees you to be exactly who you are, weaknesses and all, and never again have to pretend before him.

Then you will discover that life in God rises out of your security in his love, not your insecurity that you don't love him enough. That's the lesson Jesus wanted to teach Peter that morning by Galilee's shore. Though Peter could not answer that he loved Jesus to the depth Jesus asked, he had more to learn of the power of the cross. He had a fear of his own failures that had not been swallowed up by God's love.

This was a transforming moment for Peter, and though he couldn't get it right then, he eventually did. When he wrote his letters, the only love he spoke of toward God was the depth of love with which Jesus had addressed him. He finally tapped into a love so deep that he never needed fear again.

So can you.

Let's go to Golgotha and watch the most incredible plan ever devised unfold in all its glory.

> *You did not receive a spirit that makes you a slave again to fear, but you received the Spirit of sonship. And by him we cry, "Abba, Father."*
>
> —ROMANS 8:15

For Your Personal Journey

Are most of your actions motivated by your security in God's love for you, or your fear that if you don't do enough God might not be pleased with you? Ask him to show you the ways your fears motivate you in day-to-day decisions. Read through 1 John 4:7–21 every morning for a few days and meditate on John's words there. Ask him to help you discover how much he loves you and, in doing so, to drive out the fears in your life.

For Group Discussion

1. Today if Jesus asked you the same question he asked Peter, how would you respond?

2. What things do you do for God that seem motivated by your fear of him or his judgments against you?

3. What things do you do that seem to flow out of knowing that God loves you?

4. Compare those experiences motivated by fear and those by love. How do you feel in each circumstance?

5. Read 1 John 4:7–21 and identify the specific things John identifies about God's love.

6. Pray together that God will increasingly reveal the depth of his love for each of you.

SECTION III

The Undeniable Proof

If God is for us, who can be against us?
He who did not spare his own Son, but gave
him up for us all—how will he not also, along with
him, graciously give us all things?

—Romans 8:31–32

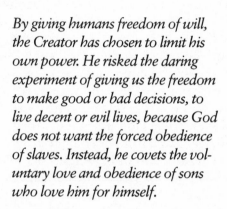

11

By giving humans freedom of will, the Creator has chosen to limit his own power. He risked the daring experiment of giving us the freedom to make good or bad decisions, to live decent or evil lives, because God does not want the forced obedience of slaves. Instead, he covets the voluntary love and obedience of sons who love him for himself.

CATHERINE MARSHALL, *BEYOND OUR SELVES*

He Loved You Enough to Let You Go

"IT WAS ABOUT OBEDIENCE, pure and simple." The words drifted over from an animated conversation two tables away in the restaurant where I was having lunch. "That's all God wanted from Adam and Eve, and they couldn't give it." The other diners nodded in approval.

How I wanted to interrupt my conversation and join theirs. I used to think that, too. All that matters to God is our obedience. Weren't we all taught that?

I've since come to discover it isn't so. Certainly God wants us to be obedient to him, and Adam and Eve would have saved us all a host of grief if they had obeyed him. But God knew their disobedience was only a symptom of something he cared about far more deeply.

Since he created us to share in the relationship that Father, Son, and Spirit have shared for all eternity, we get to engage in it the same way they do. Their unity flows from the fact that they absolutely love and trust one another. You can see it throughout Scripture in the way they talk to one another and how they act together. It only makes sense that God's invitation for us to share in that relationship would be based on that same trust.

One can obey God and yet not trust him, and in doing so miss out on a relationship with him. One cannot, however, trust God and be disobedient to him. For we shall see that all disobedience flows out of mistrust in God's nature and of his intentions toward us.

Thus the experience in the Garden wasn't to demand their obedience but to incubate their trust. He knew that the first step toward him might well be a step away from him in disobedience. He knew the lesson would be painful and costly—for him most of all—but he chose it because he desired people who would relate to him in love rather than obey him in fear. It would have been far easier to accomplish the latter, but God knew that love could flourish only where trust does, and that real trust could emerge only where people were free to reject it.

As bizarre as the actions of the father of the prodigal son might seem to us, those actions made perfect sense to Jesus. He had seen the same situation a long time before in a garden called Eden. For his Father had provided everything Adam and Eve could have ever wanted, even the freedom to live apart from him.

By doing so, he gave them the greatest of all possible gifts—the potential to enter into a free and loving relationship with the God of the universe. That they chose first to trust their own wisdom and plunge the creation into the agony of sin was less his concern than how he would use that failure to invite them back to himself.

"I'D RATHER DO IT MYSELF"

God filled Eden with luscious fruit trees of every variety, but in the middle of it he planted two special trees. The Tree of Life would impart immortality to any who ate of it. The Tree of Knowledge would open Adam's and Eve's eyes to see good and evil as God saw them. He told them they were free to eat from every tree except the Tree of Knowledge. Though its fruit would enlighten, it would also kill them.

Wouldn't it have been better if he had never created it, or at least hid it in some distant corner of the globe? Certainly its presence provided the opportunity for humankind's greatest failure and with it thousands of years of suffering in sin, pain, conflict, and disease. However, God didn't plant that tree to spell out our demise, but to allow us the freedom that would make relationship with him meaningful.

He knew that whichever way Adam and Eve chose, it would still be the first step on a journey to learn how to trust his awesome love. Regrettably, like the prodigal son, they would learn to trust God only by first trusting themselves and finding out just how misguided they were in doing so.

"You will be like God," the serpent promised them that morning as he enticed them to eat what God had forbidden. What a devastating temptation! One could want worse things than to be like God. Hadn't God already made them in his image? Wasn't his desire to invite them into a relationship with him that would make them like him? Isn't the desire to be like God the highest ideal of the Christian life?

That such a noble motive could be used for such evil should be a warning to us. For here sin is clearly unmasked. We often view sin as evil action alone and miss the nature of sin itself. At its root, sin is simply grabbing for ourselves what God has not given to us. In this realm, our best intentions can draw us into as much bondage as our most indulgent desires.

Adam and Eve's sin was not *what* they wanted, but *how* they went about getting it. Would they trust God to make them like him, or would they reach out and take it for themselves?

Is that what Jesus understood when he rejected Satan's

enticement to change stones into bread after his long fast? There was certainly nothing evil in the act itself. Nothing in the old covenant forbade it, and it would be no different from changing water into wine, which he would do a few days later. Jesus, however, trusted his Father to bring to him everything he needed. Fulfilling his own ambitions, wholesome though they may be, would take him down the same path as Adam and Eve.

He knew God's gifts are always two-edged. They can be used for his glory or abused for our ambitions. Jesus chose the former; Adam and Eve the latter. The tree that stood before them in the Garden was no symbol or loyalty test. Its fruit held real spiritual power. Those who would eat of it would see good and evil the same way God saw it; and that was exactly what happened to Adam and Eve. As soon as their teeth plunged into its fruit their eyes were opened to see good and evil; and the first thing they noticed was how evil they had become. That knowledge overwhelmed them with shame and shattered their relationship with God and each other.

A LIE EXPERTLY PLACED

All it took for the enemy to wreak such havoc in God's innocent creation was to use a well-placed lie to drive a wedge between Eve and her Creator. If you've ever been the victim of such a lie, you know how devastating it can be.

"Sara doesn't care about this fellowship anymore." In an attempt to discredit me, these words were spoken about my wife by one of the leaders in the church I was pastoring. They were far from the truth, for we had helped to plant the fellowship some fifteen years earlier, loved the people as dear friends, and had even sacrificed our lives for its good.

What made the comment sound believable was the truth in which the lie was embedded. "Wayne's been out of town for two Sundays and his wife didn't come to either Sunday morning service." While it was true that she had not been there, it was because she had been out of town helping my mother deal with the death of her mother while I was on the other side of the country. She had cleaned house, helped with the funeral, and lent her emotional support in my absence.

Nothing is more dangerous than taking that which is clearly true to prove a point that is not. Mixing a little lie with a lot of truth is like hiding cyanide in Kool-Aid. You cannot tell it's there until you drink it, but by then it is too late.

That's all the serpent needed to lull Adam and Eve into their nightmare. "You surely will not die!" was lie enough to deflect Eve's thinking (NASB). *We won't die?* she must have thought. *Then why would he tell us we would?* The enemy had his answer ready. "For God knows that in the day you eat from it your eyes will be opened, and you will be like God, knowing good and evil" (NASB).

That last sentence is true, every word of it. God did know they would become like him in knowing good and evil and said so later. But notice how sinister these words became in the context of a lie. If they weren't really going to be harmed by eating the fruit, God was forbidding it only because he didn't want them to become like him. In other words, he was holding out on them.

There's the wedge. The God who made them couldn't be trusted. He was too insecure, too threatened to let anyone else be like him. No longer certain of God's motives toward them, Adam and Eve could not trust him. Their relationship with God was now suspect; not something they valued, but something to work around to get what they were afraid God might not want for them. In other words, they acted in opposition to him, instead of in cooperation with him.

Not knowing whom to believe, they did what they thought best. Seeing how delicious the fruit looked and wanting to be wise, they ate. At the root of all sin stands the same excuse: "I know best. I can get what I want on my own and not get hurt. Who needs God after all?"

The enemy had won, at least temporarily. He had violated the purity of God's new creation and severed the relationship between God and the people he loved. We still suffer the effects of this thousands of years later. But the last word would not be the serpent's.

SOMETHING GREATER THAN OBEDIENCE

Imagine if Eve had known God well enough to trust his love for her. How would she have responded to the serpent's charges against God?

I can see her face twisted in wonderment as she tries to hold back her laughter. "Are you talking about our God? The one who walked with us in the Garden last night and who loves us so much that he has given us everything for our good? You're saying he would lie to us because he doesn't want us to be like him? Absolutely, totally impossible! Not him. We are his children, after all!" And she could have walked away without even a second thought. That's the kind of trust God wants us all to know.

If obedience had been God's only issue, don't you think he would have made the whole scenario far clearer? He told them not to eat from that tree or they would die. He didn't describe that death in detail. He could have told them how it would destroy his creation by bringing sin, disease, and relational brokenness into his world. It would cause them incredible pain, and not just for them but for all their offspring for thousands of years to come. He could have told them that all they needed to do was eat first of the Tree of Life, so that they would be eternally innocent in his presence.

But he didn't tell them. If he had they might have been obedient, but not because they trusted him. They would have obeyed only because it served their self-interest. God would merely have become a tool for their own fulfillment. Self would have still been at the center of their choice, and self would prevent them from discovering the full vitality of life in him. No, God didn't tell them because he wanted something far better.

Neither did he interrupt the serpent to set the truth firmly in mind again. After all, he was there, wasn't he? Or do you imagine him busy in heaven with his back turned at that critical moment? We know now what Adam and Eve could not know then. They recognized him only when he cloaked himself in some physical manifestation and walked the Garden with them. They didn't know that this God was present everywhere in his creation.

So why didn't he intervene? Could it be the same reason Jesus didn't send Peter home instead of letting him follow along to Caiaphas's courtyard and the betrayal that would devastate him? God sees something redemptive even in letting us fail. He seems less concerned about our mistakes than how we respond to them. Do our mistakes lead us away from trusting in our own strength or wisdom and toward seeking what it means to put our trust in him?

If so, then he finds even our failures worth the pain they cause.

THE FINAL WORD

I'm sure the father of the prodigal son could sit on the porch after his boy had returned, thinking that the money squandered in sin was well spent if it brought his son to the end of himself and into the relationship the father had always wanted with him. As painful as it was to watch, it had helped his son realize exactly what kind of father he had.

God could have helped Adam and Eve make the right decision, certainly. But he wanted something else far more—to awaken the trust that would allow them to participate in the divine community. What an incredible plan! God provided a choice for them that was obviously in their self-interest, but he framed it in a way that seeking their own desires would lead them to the wrong choice. Only by learning to trust him would they experience the deepest longing of their hearts.

But Eden was not the final word. It was only the first of many lessons. The familiar proverb advises that if you love something, you should set it free. If it comes back to you, it's yours. If it doesn't, it never was. Only those who have loved something enough to let it go can even get a glimpse of what God accomplished in that Garden.

God loved us that much, and, though many in the course of history have not come back, many others have. Somehow the pain of those who do not is swallowed up in the joy of those who do. Thus the tragedy in the Garden becomes a stepping-stone to the greater good he desired. In the midst of sin and selfishness, he would use our own waywardness and its consequences as the incubator in which our trust in his love might yet emerge.

That day began a process that would culminate at another tree—this one a cross on the hill at Golgotha. There mercy would triumph over sin; and the trust that had been so elusive in that Garden for Adam and Eve would become certain for those who belong to God.

> *If, by the trespass of the one man, death reigned through that one man, how much more will those who receive God's abundant provision of grace and of the gift of righteousness reign in life through the one man, Jesus Christ.*
>
> —ROMANS 5:17

For Your Personal Journey

Ask God to reveal to you where wedges of mistrust have been inserted between you and him. Where do you find yourself doubting his love for you or his intentions with you? Where has trusting in your own abilities and wisdom taken you further from him rather than closer to him? Ask God to show you how to embrace a relationship with him in his way and not your own.

For Group Discussion

1. Explain and discuss the following: one can obey without trusting, but one cannot trust without obeying.

2. Think of some moments in your life when your efforts to do good only backfired and made the situation worse.

3. What kinds of things does the enemy whisper in your ear to drive a wedge between you and God so that your trust in him is eroded?

4. What do you think God can do to help you trust him more?

12

*Church! Why would
I ever go there? I was
already feeling terrible
about myself. They'd just
make me feel worse!*

A PROSTITUTE FROM CHICAGO
AS QUOTED BY PHILIP YANCEY
IN *WHAT'S SO AMAZING ABOUT
GRACE?*

Who Needed the Sacrifice?

"FOR GOD SO LOVED the world that he gave his one and only Son, that whoever believes in him shall not perish but have eternal life" (John 3:16).

Am I the only one who didn't think this Scripture was such great news the first time I heard it? Yes, I know it speaks of an incredible gift God gave so that we would not have to perish for our sins. For us, it is undoubtedly a great thing. But what does it say about God?

When I heard this in Sunday school as a child, my first response was, "If he loved us so much, why didn't he do it himself?" Admittedly I might have been influenced by the chores I had to do at home: for Dad so loved a well-kept

yard that he sent me out to mow it. Dad so loved his vineyard that he sent me to work in it. Dad so loved an ice-cold
Pepsi that he sent me to the refrigerator to get it for him.

So why didn't God himself appear in human flesh and
submit himself to the most painful and humiliating death
imaginable? No, he sent the Son instead; or so I used to
think. And my confusion didn't end there. While I was
grateful for the salvation he provided, I had some concerns
about God because of the way he provided it.

What kind of Father satisfies his need for justice by the
death of his own Son? Couldn't he have just forgiven us
without taking it out on an innocent victim? If someone
wronged me and the only way I could satisfy my anger was
to punish someone else as the means to forgive them, what
would that say about me?

If the cross served God's need to be appeased by a human
sacrifice, especially that of his own Son, we are left with a
host of disturbing questions. Raise them with others, and
most will escape answering them by claiming that God's
demand for justice is beyond our comprehension. But I am
convinced the dissonant perspectives about God that result
from an appeasement-based view of the cross cause many to
shy away from the intimate relationship he seeks with us.

Instead, the unanswerable questions should invite us to
reconsider our distorted view of the cross. Since Adam's
fall we have come to picture God not as a loving Father
inviting us to trust him, but as an exacting sovereign who
must be appeased. When we start from that vantage point
we miss God's purpose of the cross. For his plan was not
to satisfy some need in himself at his Son's expense, but
rather to satisfy a need in us at his own expense.

THE COVER-UP

Living by appeasement is a frightful game, especially when
you play it with the all-knowing, almighty God. Though I
don't believe for a moment that God plays it, many of us

were taught that he does, and, thus, we alternate between trying to do enough to please him and trying to hide from him when we realize we can't.

The moment Adam and Eve ate the fruit, their eyes were opened to see good and evil. The first evil they saw was in themselves. Though they had been naked since they were created, now they were aware of their nakedness and sought to cover their shame.

Evidently the first things they saw that were big enough to cover them were fig leaves. They plucked a few, sewed them together, and slipped them on. I cringe at the thought. I've been in fig orchards and know how prickly and itchy those leaves are. As material for underwear it was a poor choice indeed, as are most of the ways we try to cover ourselves.

But the real price of their shame was seen a short while later as God revealed himself again in the Garden. Instead of feeling safe with him, they felt compelled to hide from him. Notice that God neither hid from them nor was he angry at their disobedience. Instead, he just showed up to be with them. They were the ones cowering in shame, hoping the bushes would cover what their fig leaves couldn't.

As God came closer they told him of their shame and their failure. In doing so, they still sought cover. Adam blamed Eve: "The woman . . . gave me some fruit from the tree, and I ate it." No wonder they felt unsafe in their nakedness. They were. He turned on her to justify himself, using blame for the same purpose he had used fig leaves.

Adam's blame didn't stop at Eve. It was not just the woman who tripped him up, but "the woman you put here with me." Adam even tried to pass some of the responsibility on to God. When God turned his attention to Eve, she blamed the serpent's deception.

The creation was stained, and God parceled out the consequences of that failure. Already spiritually dead in the relational brokenness that resulted, their future physical death would follow. God threw them out of his Garden because he did not want them to eat from the Tree of Life and live forever in that sinful condition. By preserving eternity in holiness, God prepared a safe haven for their eventual rescue. "The soul who sins is the one who will die" is a proclamation of mercy, not anger. It means that sin must have an end, and we an opportunity to regain what we forfeited.

TERMS OF APPEASEMENT

Adam and Eve's failure had profound consequences in the creation and in their relationship to their Creator. He could no longer be the Friend who walked with them in the Garden because their own sense of shame would cause them to cower whenever he approached.

Knowing good and evil didn't provide the joy Adam and Eve thought it would. Because they came to know good and evil outside their trust in God, they had no power to resist evil and choose the good. They, as have all generations after them, found themselves captive to evil passions, with destructive consequences and the overwhelming sense of shame.

When God did make himself known, even the most righteous people fell on their faces, overwhelmed by their own unworthiness. The friendship he desired with his creation was thwarted. Instead of seeking his friendship, people thought only to appease him—doing enough good to somehow convince themselves that they were worthy of his favor. The Creator had become someone to avoid, not to embrace.

Shame so permeates our nature that this appeasement-based approach has emerged in every false religion devised by humanity. From the earliest tribal attempts to appease the "gods of the earth" or the "god of rain," to more sophisticated religious systems with idolatry and tradition, the objective has always been the same: what can we do to appease the wrath of the gods and curry their favor?

He loves me. He loves me not.

Good times lead to complacency and bad times to even greater rituals of repentant prayers, sacrificial offerings, and good deeds. Offerings started with small gestures of fruits or grain, but increasingly difficult times demanded ever-greater gifts. Soon animals were sacrificed, and eventually in many cultures throughout the world human sacrifice became the ultimate expression of commitment to a god.

But this is not how the only true God wanted to be known.

I WILL PROVIDE MY OWN

If you go to Tel Megiddo in Israel today, you can stand on an overlook and view an altar used to sacrifice firstborn male children to the gods of the Canaanites. Your guide will tell you that very altar was in use when Abraham entered the Promised Land. People thought they could appease their false gods with such sacrifices.

Thus it was not so incredible to Abraham when the God who had touched his life asked him to sacrifice his only son. All the other gods in Canaan did it, why not his? But this God was not a false god like the others deemed interested in human sacrifice. This was the true God. He was going to reveal himself to Abraham and wanted him to know this God had nothing in common with Molech, Baal, or Asherah.

At God's instruction, Abraham took his son—a treasure born in his old age—and set out for Mount Moriah. As they got close to the mountain, Isaac noticed that they had no sacrifice. "The fire and wood are here, . . . but where is the lamb for the burnt offering?"

It appears that Abraham's response was less a brilliant insight into God's nature than a deflection to stave off the curiosity of his son. He nonetheless spoke prophetically the lesson God wanted to show him: "God himself will provide the lamb for the burnt offering, my son."

Only later, after his son lay tied to the altar and Abraham lifted the knife to plunge it into his son, did he see just how prophetic his words were: "The angel of the LORD called out to him from heaven, 'Abraham! Abraham! Do not lay a hand on the boy. . . . Do not do anything to him. Now I know that you fear God, because you have not withheld from me your son, your only son'" (Gen. 22:12).

Abraham had faced the ultimate test in his growing trust in God. Even though he was willing to sacrifice Isaac, he discovered that God really didn't want or need the sacrifice. After God pointed out to Abraham a ram caught nearby in the bushes, he offered it in Isaac's place. Abraham named that place "The LORD Will Provide," understanding that his earlier words had proved more true than he could have imagined at the time.

In this one act God drew a line that separated him from all the false gods men had ever created. The false gods demanded sacrifices for their own appeasement. This God provided the sacrifice we needed to finally cover our shame and allow us to know him as he really is.

At Mount Moriah God foreshadowed to Abraham what he would literally accomplish some three thousand years later on another hill not far away, Golgotha. It would not be the act of appeasement to an angry God by any sacrifice we could give, but an act of a loving God to sacrifice himself for those who were held captive in sin.

Far from being a bloodthirsty sovereign demanding sacrifice to satiate his need for vengeance, the living God spent himself to bring back the banished son or daughter. He did not need a sacrifice to love us, for he already did love us.

We needed a sacrifice for our shame so that we would be free to love him again. At the cross, God provided the undeniable proof of just how much he loves us. Understanding that opens the door for us to do what Adam and Eve could not do that fateful day in the Garden—totally entrust our lives to the living God.

> *There is now no condemnation for those who are in Christ Jesus, because through Christ Jesus the law of the Spirit of life set me free from the law of sin and death.*
>
> —ROMANS 8:1–2

For Your Personal Journey

Can you recognize the effects of shame in your own life? What effort will you expend to make yourself look better to others, to yourself, or even to God? In your relationship with God, do you think more of what you have to do for him or what he has already done for you? Ask him to show you how appeasement distorts your relationship with him, and ask him to free you from it so that you can participate in what he wants to do in you.

For Group Discussion

1. Reflect together on the truth that the true God is the one who wants to sacrifice for us instead of demanding our sacrifices for him.

2. Where do you still try to appease God in the sacrifices you make or in blaming others to alleviate your guilt?

3. How does this change the way you view Christianity?

4. Spend some moments thanking God for providing all you need to come into a trusting relationship with him.

13

*I had totally misun-
derstood the Chris-
tian faith. I came
to see that it was in
my brokenness and
powerlessness, in my
weakness that Jesus
was made strong.
It was in the accep-
tance of my lack of
faith that God could
give me faith.*

MIKE YACONELLI, QUOTED
IN BRENNAN MANNING,
ABBA'S CHILD

The Hen and
Her Chicks

WHEN I FIRST HEARD THE STORY, I was told it was
from an issue of *National Geographic*. I've learned since
that it never appeared there and is probably an urban
legend. Whether or not this has actually happened among
birds in the wild, something very much like it happened
one afternoon just outside ancient Jerusalem.

Allegedly a group of firefighters were checking up on
hot spots after a forest fire had been contained. As they
marched across the blackened landscape between the
wisps of smoke still rising from the smoldering vegetation,
a large lump on the trail caught one firefighter's eye.

As he got closer he noticed it was the charred remains

of a large bird. Since birds can so easily fly away from the approaching flames, the firefighter wondered what was wrong with this bird that it could not escape. Had it been sick or injured?

Arriving at the carcass, he decided to kick it off the trail with his boot. As he did, however, he was startled by a flurry of activity around his feet. Four little birds flailed in the dust and ash, then scurried down the hillside.

The bulk of the mother's body had covered them from the searing flames. Though the heat was enough to consume her, it allowed her babies to find safety underneath. In the face of the rising flames, she had stayed with her young. She was their only hope for safety, and, willing to risk her own life, she had gathered them together and covered them with her own body. Even when the encroaching flames began to scorch her feathers, she could easily have flown away to start another family on another day. How did she make herself stay in the raging flames?

Her dead carcass and her fleeing chicks told the story well enough—she gave the ultimate sacrifice to save her young. Whether or not this has ever truly been duplicated in creation, it illustrates an even greater reality. For the Creator of heaven and earth did exactly the same thing to rescue his wayward children from their own destruction.

THE WORST CURSE

Jesus found himself surrounded by his most hostile audience. No one gave him more trouble than the elders and Pharisees in Jerusalem. Their only priority seemed to be protecting their position in society and trying to deal with this miracle-working Teacher with a mix of personal disdain one moment and feigned support the next when they were afraid of the people. They were disingenuous to the core, always covering up their real motives and actions to act out a holiness they did not possess.

In his final words to the city of Jerusalem only days before his death, Jesus exposed the scribes and Pharisees for what they really were—hypocrites who turned the work of the loving God into a religion they manipulated for their own gain and sense of self-importance. He pronounced eight curses or "woes" on them, and five times he called them "blind" (NASB).

He exposed them for keeping people from the reality of the kingdom, for loving their titles of respect and chief seats in their meetings, for making converts they lured only into greater bondage, for skewed priorities, for pretending to be righteous on the outside when evil raged within, for glorifying the prophets of the past and rejecting the prophets of their day.

The last charge was serious indeed. "You brood of vipers," Jesus called them. "How will you escape the sentence of hell?" (NASB). In the days ahead God would send his messengers to them again, but they would torture and kill them. Jesus warned them that because of their deeds they would be held responsible for "all the righteous blood that has been shed on earth."

What a curse! Jesus would hold them accountable for the blood of every righteous person since the day Cain slew his brother, Abel. He could already see the consequences bearing down on them like a firestorm of wrath, seeking to consume them in their sin.

Don't these words seem completely out of character for Jesus? His message of love and forgiveness had captivated the land, drawing to him some of the most sinful people of his day. Yet these religious leaders he condemned in the cruelest of terms. Had he utterly rejected them?

That's how it appears on the surface, but look closer. Rather than taking delight in their coming devastation, he offered his life to rescue them from it. In words both poetic and poignant, he made them an incredible offer.

UNDER HIS WINGS

O Jerusalem, Jerusalem, you who kill the prophets and stone those sent to you, how often I have longed

to gather your children together, as a hen gathers her
chicks under her wings, but you were not willing.
—Matthew 23:37

They had rejected God and the messengers he had sent. They had earned the harshest of sentences for their actions, and yet Jesus still wanted to draw them to him and bear the destruction for them. Their city would be conquered and their children devastated by the consequences of living selfishly instead of trusting in the living God.

Jesus invoked the image of a mother bird protecting her children with her own body. He pictured himself as a hen trying to gather chicks to herself, which happens only when danger presses in upon them. A hen doesn't nurse her children or cuddle them to sleep. But when a predator comes near or the coop catches on fire, she will try to gather them under her wings. Pulling them beneath her, she will put her own body between them and the danger, risking her own life for their safety.

Jesus could see the firestorm the people's own sin had produced as he approached Jerusalem. It would devour them utterly. Even though many in that crowd would cry for his crucifixion only a few days later, he still wanted to save them. Like the hen, he offered them a safe place under his wings, willing to endure the fire to the point of death to rescue whoever wanted to come.

When it would have been so easy for him to abandon them to the fate they deserved, he was going to stay and meet the approaching fire in its full fury. What must it take for a bird to stay over her babies as the fire draws ever closer, then begins to sear her neck and back? What must it have taken for God himself to endure the fury of wrath our sins deserved and endure it to the end so that those under his wings might be saved?

"But you were not willing." The story's end was tragic for those who stood around Jesus that day. Unwilling to come to him, they would have to endure the fire themselves to its tragic end. I doubt there are words that break the

Father's heart more than these. After all he had done to deliver them from the ravages of sin, they were unwilling.

Not all chicks run to their mothers in times of danger. Some, either paralyzed in panic or trying to find a way to save themselves, are devoured. She cannot run around gathering them individually. They have to come to her. That's all the young chicks in the forest fire had done to be safe. They didn't have to earn it; all they had to do was run under the mother's wing and let her cover them.

Those who did were rescued; those who didn't were devoured. It didn't matter if they thought they had a better idea. It didn't matter if they thought they could outrun it. All that mattered was their willingness to trust the call of their mother.

Most of Jerusalem on that day would not accept Jesus' call and would face the terrible judgment ahead on their own terms. But the story doesn't have to end that way for you. For God's wrath will still come to consume the sin out of his creation. If you want, you can give up all the ways you try to save yourself and come running to him. He will pull you up close, under his wing, and take for you what you could never endure.

UNLIMITED PATIENCE

Look how closely our choice in Christ parallels Adam and Eve's choice in the Garden. If they had trusted their Creator's love for them, they would not have resorted to their own means to become like God. Once they doubted his love for them, they could only fall back on their best wisdom, which proved woefully inadequate.

The elders in Jerusalem faced a similar choice. Would they trust their own religious ways to save themselves, or would they trust God's work in Jesus? Remember, these were not self-indulgent men fulfilling their passions by outwardly sinful acts. No, the deception for them was much like it was for Adam and Eve. These were men trying to be godly, or so they thought. They observed cumbersome rituals and traditions thinking that would make them like God. They spurned the pleasures of the world in an effort to earn his approval. But being good wasn't good enough.

They were still engaged in an attempt to save themselves, and they would end up in the same mess as Adam and Eve. No matter how righteous they could be on the outside, it would bring them no closer to God. They were still trusting themselves instead of him. Unfortunately, many who are caught up in the religion Christianity has become have fallen for the same lie.

Jesus unmasked their deception most clearly when he called one of their own to himself. Paul, formerly called Saul, had grown up training to be a Pharisee. Everything about his life conformed to their code, such that Paul could later say that no one was his equal in zeal for God, and as for legalistic righteousness, he was faultless. With such impressive credentials, you would think him well-placed for God's work.

Rubbish! That's what Paul called that way of thinking. It was boasting in the flesh, he said, and that flesh had not saved him. It had only driven his sin ever deeper underground. Though he appeared to be one of the most righteous men in his day, in reality he was full of sin. He called himself the worst of sinners because his religious exterior had only been a cover-up for the sin that destroyed him from within. He called himself a "blasphemer and a persecutor and a violent man."

Don't mistake his assessment here as the mere humility of a gracious man. Paul was trying to convince all who would listen that self-righteousness is no righteousness at all. Driven by his desire to be one of the spiritual elite of his day, he had only found himself in greater sin. When Jesus found him, he was in fact killing God's people, thinking he was doing God's work. He was the Osama bin Laden of his day.

Why did Jesus save Paul? In Paul's words, "I was shown mercy so that in me, the worst of sinners, Christ Jesus might display his unlimited patience as an example for those who would believe on him and receive eternal life" (1 Tim. 1:16).

I've sat with people convinced they were far too evil for God to want them. I've often referred to this passage, asking them if they had done worse than Paul had done, and I haven't ever had people tell me they had. God saved Paul so the most broken, devastated, and sinful person would feel free to come running under his wing. All that person has to do is come.

A REAL COVERING

When God put Adam and Eve out of the Garden, he even looked in mercy at their cover-up. Taking the undergarments they had fashioned from the fig leaf collection, he made them clothing of animal skins. It was not only an act of mercy, but also prophetic demonstration. The blood shed to cover them that day testified to a future day when Jesus' death would provide the covering we really need.

Shame craves a covering. We've already seen how it can reveal itself in blaming others, even God, for our own choices and weaknesses. Now we see how shame can use religion as a cover-up as well. Instead of being known for who we are, we protect ourselves by pretending to be what we are not. That's why relationships in religious environments can turn so painful when people have to tear others down to make themselves look better.

We push to achieve beyond our peers so we can feel superior to them. We blame others so we don't have to face our own weaknesses. We gossip about the failures of others so we can feel better about ourselves. We even look for religious institutions to affirm us so that we can ignore the doubts that assail us.

It seems we all are on the relentless pursuit to hide our own inadequacies and seek our own security. In doing so, we are like little chickens running around the burning coop, throwing leaves over our heads and hoping they will be enough shelter.

But they won't be. There is only one covering that will save us from ourselves, and it is Jesus himself. He has already endured the firestorm for us so that those who crawl under his wings can dwell in safety. He is the only covering that at once delivers us from our shame and frees us from the bondage of sin.

Cover yourself in him. Learn to live under his wings today and every day for the rest of your life. How do you do that? By coming to rest in the security of his love for you, allowing it to hold you in the most brutal of circumstances.

Of course that is far easier said than done. When difficulties press in around us, we are most likely to doubt God's motives toward us. Could that be the voice of the serpent still whispering in our ears? "If God's not going to give you what you think you need, maybe you should go get it yourself." Or perhaps he uses Ben Franklin's words: "God helps those who help themselves."

Trusting our own wisdom is so easy we find ourselves doing it before we ever realize it. There is only one place where we can learn the trust in God that was shattered in Eden—at the cross of Jesus Christ. His willingness to trade his life for ours stands as unmistakable evidence of his love for us.

When you understand what really happened there, you will know how much you are loved. When you know how much you're loved, you'll find trusting him to be as easy as breathing.

> *May I never boast except in the cross of our Lord Jesus Christ, through which the world has been crucified to me, and I to the world.*
>
> —GALATIANS 6:14

For Your Personal Journey

Where do you try to save yourself using your own ingenuity to survive, rather than trusting Jesus to lead you as he desires? Isn't his unlimited patience amazing in that even after our worst deeds, he stands ready to cover us with his wings and let us abide safely in him? Ask him to show you what that means specifically for you and to teach you how to live every day and through every circumstance trusting that he loves you.

For Group Discussion

1. What did you get out of the story of the hen and her chicks?

2. Have you ever used religion as a covering for shame? How?

3. What is easier for you to do, run under his wing or try to figure out a way to fix things yourself? Why do you think that is?

4. Give examples of God's unlimited patience and celebrate together in prayer his awesome faithfulness to the weakest of his people.

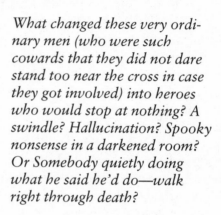

14

What changed these very ordinary men (who were such cowards that they did not dare stand too near the cross in case they got involved) into heroes who would stop at nothing? A swindle? Hallucination? Spooky nonsense in a darkened room? Or Somebody quietly doing what he said he'd do—walk right through death?

J. B. PHILLIPS, *IS GOD AT HOME?*

What Really Happened on the Cross

THE EVENTS ON EARTH have been well documented. All of the writers of the Gospels tell of Jesus' inquisition before the religious leaders of Jerusalem, his trial before Pilate, his scourging by Roman soldiers, and his crucifixion on a cross. The humiliation and physical torture of death by crucifixion have been the subject of many sermons and books. We know well the agony he endured by being nailed to a cross with a crown of thorns pressed into his scalp, and we also know how his agony intensified over the three hours he hung exposed to public view, mocked by his detractors.

The significance of that moment, however, is not so easy to understand. The appeasement-based view of the cross that most of us have understood goes something like this: Because Jesus lived a sinless life, he did not deserve to die. However, he submitted himself to his Father's desire, and as a sacrifice he accepted the guilt of our sins. Then God punished him to satisfy the justice our sins deserved. By enduring our sentence, Jesus absolved the guilt of our sins and we can now stand justified before the holy God.

Though this scenario may satisfy our inherent sense of shame for our own sins and failures, it tells only part of the story. If we go no further, this appeasement-based view of the cross describes Father and Son playing a divine version of good cop/bad cop. To keep the demanding Judge of the universe from executing the full weight of his wrath on us, Jesus rushed to the scene and threw himself in the way. God's wrath destroyed him and thus mollified his anger.

But that is only an earthly view of that incredible event. Scripture is laced with glimpses at a far fuller perspective. Here we see what happened *in God*—the work a Father and Son accomplished together, not to appease God's anger, but to cleanse us of sin. Their plan was not merely to punish sin, but to destroy its power and offer a way for humanity to be rescued from the brokenness of sin to recapture the relationship God had always wanted with his people.

What we see from his vantage point is not just the story of the punishment of an undeserving victim, but something far more glorious.

NOT JUST A VICTIM

Yes, Jesus was brutally tortured, and it was certainly the intent of the Roman guard that the extreme tortures used against him would end his life. That, however, is not the whole story. Nothing they could do would have been sufficient to kill the Son.

Jesus was neither a victim of the lies of the religious rulers nor a victim of Rome's corrupt political posturing. No amount of torture would have been sufficient to kill him. Death would come only when he surrendered to it. "The reason my Father loves me is that I lay down my life. . . . No one takes it from me, but I lay it down of my own accord" (John 10:17–18).

The cross alone could not kill Jesus. Only the soul that sins, dies. Since Jesus knew no sin, death could not overpower him. Instead, he submitted to death for a greater good. He didn't just submit to the events of the cross, but even at its end he yielded his spirit into God's hands and gave himself over to death.

Neither Adam and Eve in the Garden nor Christ on the cross were victims of other people's choices. In the pristine beauty of the undefiled creation, Adam and Eve couldn't find it in their hearts to trust God and walk away from their own desires. But in the agonizing atrocity of the cross and the utter darkness that overwhelmed him there, Jesus consciously and continuously yielded to his Father's desire.

At any point in the process he could have stopped the torture, called for a legion of angels, and wiped out those who were killing him. What an amazing act! I don't know that I have ever willingly submitted to the darkest tragedies of my life. I rarely feel in control when circumstances turn desperate or when people with evil motives take advantage of me. If I could have called a legion of angels to fix any of my painful circumstances, I would have. I have endured the painful seasons of my life not because I chose to, but because I could not do otherwise. The only choice I had was whether to respond to them in a godly way or a selfish way.

That Jesus would endure such hostility against himself with the full freedom to end it at any weak moment makes me appreciate the cross that much more. As free choice got us into this bondage of sin, so Jesus' free choice would walk us out of it. His example also reminds us that we are not victims either. Even though disgusting things might be done to us by others, we still have the freedom to overcome evil by putting our trust in him. He still redeems the darkest moments of life with the wonder of his grace.

NOT JUST JESUS . . .

I'll be the first to admit that the relationship of Father, Son, and Spirit is a mystery beyond our ability to define with absolute certainty. But I am deeply bothered by the thought that in some way God was able to separate himself at the cross. The popular understanding of the cross is that God the Father executed wrath on God the Son while standing at some discrete distance.

Such thinking not only denies the essence of God's nature but also distorts the facts of the cross. Paul wrote that "God was reconciling the world to himself in Christ." God was no distant observer, but a participant. He didn't send Jesus to do what he would not do, but God himself acted through Jesus to bring about our redemption.

Some have taken Jesus' cry that his Father had forsaken him to mean that at the darkest moment, the Father had to turn his back on the Son. God cannot bear to look on sin, they argue, so that when our sins were laid on him, God had to turn his face away from his Son.

God has never run from sinful humanity. He didn't hide from Adam and Eve in the Garden. *They* hid from him as *he* sought them out. It is not that God cannot bear to look on sin, but that we in our sin can't bear to look on God. He's not the one who hides. We are. God is powerful enough to look on sin and be untainted by it. He has always done so. He did so at the cross.

In chapter 16 we'll take a closer look at why Jesus cried out, "My God, my God, why have you forsaken me?" My point here is that all of God was fully involved in all aspects of this incredible plan. The anguish that ripped through the Godhead that day cannot even be fathomed by our limited perspective.

But it is important that we see them working together, enduring the process necessary to destroy sin and liberate those they love. Jesus was not the victim and his Father the victimizer. They were executing a plan they—the Father, Son, and Spirit—had devised on the day they first decided to create a man and a woman. They would pay the price together for the relationship they so deeply desired to share with us.

NOT JUST GUILTY OF SIN

God made him who had no sin to be sin for us, so that in him we might become the righteousness of God.
—2 CORINTHIANS 5:21

To say that God laid the guilt of our sins on Jesus so that he could punish him misses the larger point. Jesus wasn't just guilty of our sins; he *became* sin itself. Notice the word is in the singular, not talking about the *acts* of sin, but the very root of it—that self-preferring, self-trusting nature that puts itself above God.

Paul wrote that in a moment in time God made Jesus the personification of sin. While that may appear only as a minor subpoint at first glance, it is critical if we are going to understand what really happened on that cross. He didn't just deal with our sins, but with the very nature of sin itself.

By allowing sin to touch his person through the Son, he would be able to prevail in himself over that which we were powerless to fight. Through the physical body of Jesus, sin came face-to-face with the power of God, and, as we shall see, God prevailed over sin completely.

This underscores the fallacy of any law-based or performance-based approach to God. Jesus became sin for us precisely because we were powerless to deal with it ourselves. Scripture is clear here. If any of us could have been righteous on our own, then there would have been no need for Jesus to die. When we fell into sin in a state of unbelief in who God was, sin became an inescapable trap. We couldn't win over it without trust, and we couldn't trust while blinded by sin.

Thus God took sin into himself through the physical body of Jesus and accomplished what the law never could—"He condemned sin in sinful man" (Rom. 8:3). Notice it's not sinful people who were condemned, but the sin within them. The reason we are free from condemnation in Jesus is because he already bore that condemnation. It could not prevail over God's power, and by breaking its power, he opened the door for all who want to be set free of it and live in the life of the Father.

NOT JUST PUNISHMENT

Notice how God's perspective doesn't focus on our sins as much as it focuses on the power of sin itself. This is critical. For the cross was not just an act of punishment for sin. It wasn't just Jesus stepping forward as an innocent victim to take our place on the gallows. Certainly that image does express some of what happened, but punishment alone doesn't break the power of sin.

We see that in our own society. Children punished for wrongdoing often only find a better way to hide it next time or, despite their best efforts, fall victim to it again. So many people who serve jail time for an offense find themselves back again within a short time of being freed. Don't we all know that the desires of our flesh are often stronger than the threat of punishment or negative consequence?

No, the cross was not primarily about exacting punishment; it was about prevailing over sin's power. In the Son, God didn't just punish sin, he served up the antidote that Christ was able to endure until sin itself was destroyed.

Now, all who embrace him can live in the effects of that antidote, prevailing over sin through a growing relationship with the Creator of all.

> *This is love: not that we loved God, but that he loved us and sent his Son as an atoning sacrifice for our sins.*
> —1 JOHN 4:10

For Your Personal Journey

What comes first to your mind as you contemplate the death of Jesus? Think beyond the physical realities and see what transpired between Father and Son as they provided a safe place for you from the destruction of sin itself. There is nothing more to do here than to simply express to God your gratefulness for providing such an incredible gift.

For Group Discussion

1. Together share how the story of the cross has touched your life. What events stick out in your mind?

2. What do you see going on between the Father and the Son through those moments?

3. What does it mean to you that Jesus became sin itself? Share your ideas.

4. Read one of the Crucifixion accounts and give thanks together for the indescribable lengths to which God went so that we might have life in his name.

15

*If you love deeply,
you're going to
get hurt badly.
But it's still
worth it.*

C. S. LEWIS,
SHADOWLANDS

The Antidote for Sin

IT WAS THE MOST POIGNANT PICTURE OF WRATH I've witnessed. I had taken my family camping in the Sierra Nevada mountains to escape the heat of our home on the valley floor and to enjoy some rest and relaxation. I was hunkered down in a lounge chair deeply engrossed in a novel. My wife, Sara, was coming to join me when suddenly we heard screams of pain from our two-year-old son, Andy.

He'd been playing in the dirt not far from our campsite. As I looked up he was stomping his feet and waving his hands wildly. Swirling around him were flying insects, backlit by the sun; Sara immediately recognized them as bees. Somehow he had stumbled into their nest in the ground and they were attacking him relentlessly.

Before I could extricate myself from the reclining chair, Sara was rushing to the sounds of his screams. Even though she is allergic to beestings and got stung for her efforts, she angrily swatted at the bees as she scooped up her son to run with him to safety. When I got to them she was stroking his head with comfort even as she was panting from the overload of adrenaline still coursing through her veins. Soon she reacted to the venom and we took her to the hospital for treatment.

If you want a picture of God's wrath, I can think of none better. She was as angry as I've ever seen her, but the anger wasn't directed at Andy, nor did it seek punishment. She simply risked herself to rescue someone she loved so deeply.

THE WRATH OF GOD

That's what God's wrath is like. He sees the evil that mars his creation and destroys the people he loves, and he must rid us of it. His wrath consumes evil and wickedness and as such does not exist as the opposite of his love, but as an expression of that love. He must protect and set free the object of his affection.

I'm sure when my son first saw his mom running at him, eyes blazing with anger, he thought he was in trouble. Even though he didn't know what he'd done wrong, he was already recoiling from her as she approached. Only after she had swept him to safety did he realize he was not the focus of her anger, but its beneficiary.

Our shame-consciousness does the same thing toward God. Whenever we see God acting to consume sin, we internalize the anger against ourselves. But that isn't where the wrath is primarily directed. "The wrath of God is being revealed from heaven against all the godlessness and wickedness of men" (Rom. 1:18).

It's not people God seeks to destroy but the sin that destroys his people. In that sense God's wrath is far more curative than it is punitive. Its primary purpose is not to hurt us, but to heal and to redeem us.

That's not to say God's wrath doesn't ultimately devour people as well. Often in the Scriptures, God's consuming presence spelled the end of people's lives when His need to deal with their sin for a larger purpose overwhelmed their humanity. Wrath, therefore, as it consumed sin also consumed the people who had become so ensnared by sin they were no longer interested in reaching out to God's mercy.

Israel occupied the Promised Land only because the nations before them had been so given over to evil that they were unredeemable. That's why God didn't give the land to Abraham but waited until the full measure of their sin had been realized. Then he gave it to the children of Israel.

Isn't it interesting that at the end of Revelation, even those who knew they had dishonored the living God cursed him instead of repenting? It seems God will use the catastrophic events of the last days to so polarize society that all those who would come to him will have full opportunity to do so. And those who don't will not be able to claim later that they had no idea who he was.

Notice that the purpose of this wrath is to consume sin and cleanse the universe. That's what it does; first inside us if we'll let it but, if not, it will do away with us. For sin must be consumed by wrath.

THE CUP JESUS DID NOT WANT

"My Father, if it is possible, may this cup be taken from me." This was the heart of Jesus' agonizing request he repeatedly prayed in his own garden on the eve of his crucifixion. The words are interesting. What cup was he talking about?

Certainly he could simply have used "cup" as a metaphor for the difficult circumstances that lay ahead of him. But Scripture also speaks about God's wrath being in a cup that is consumed by those who have been devoured by sin. Perhaps a verse from Revelation expresses it best. Those who worship the beast will "drink of the wine of God's fury, which has been poured full strength into the cup of his wrath" (Rev. 14:10).

Could this be the cup Jesus resisted that evening? Could the thought of being the object of his own Father's wrath have been so unbearable to contemplate that he sought another means to effect salvation? I don't know that it is so, for Scripture does not say it in so many words, but I think it is likely.

If it is God's wrath that consumes sin, and if the redemptive plan was to consume sin in sinful flesh, then it could be that Jesus drank from that same cup. This would have made the physical tortures of the cross pale in comparison. In those hours he hung on the cross, he drank from God's cup so that the wrath of God might condemn sin in the Son.

Thus God's wrath is not just punishment for sin, it is also the antidote for it. Because sin was destroyed, the door to a future world without it was opened. As God's wrath will eventually purge the world of sin, so it could also purge the sin in us. The only problem is that in our fallen state, God's wrath would consume us before it would consume our sin. For us it's a case of the cure being worse than the disease. Whenever God's wrath broke out in the Old Testament to consume sin, people died! The flesh was too weak to withstand the cleansing.

But before the beginning of the world, Father and Son had together devised a plan that could redeem the object of their affection.

DRINKING THE CUP

What if you had a young child who was diagnosed with a rare blood disease? The doctors tell you that the disease is almost unheard of in children. Though they have a form of chemotherapy that could cleanse your child's blood and restore him to health, the drug is too strong for the child's undeveloped body to withstand the dose necessary to cure him. In other words, the cure would kill him before it healed him.

But there is a way around that, they say. They could transplant his blood into your own. You would then contract the disease and they could administer the chemotherapy into your blood. Though it would make you excruciatingly ill and eventually kill you, the therapy would produce antigens in your blood that could then be transplanted to your child's body and cleanse him of his disease. Would you do it? Most parents wouldn't hesitate for a second.

Neither did God. This was his opportunity to destroy the power of sin and liberate those who had been captives to it all their lives. The onlookers at Golgotha that day saw only a man experiencing the agonizing death of crucifixion. They did not know that the Sinless One had been made into sin for them and that the physical pains of the cross only reflected in human terms what transpired in God's eternity.

It seems that the cup of wrath was lifted to his lips and Jesus drank of it fully, letting it eat away at sin itself. He drank it to the end, letting wrath war against sin until sin succumbed to the power of God and was consumed in him.

How can we even imagine the battle that ravaged his soul during those hours? We have glimpses of it certainly, but only that. Jesus not only entered the utter depths of the pain, darkness, shame, and anguish to which sin can drive humanity, but he also endured the full weight of God's being warring against that sin to its utter destruction.

The first we can relate to in part because we all have tasted of sin and its painful and destructive consequences. The latter we will never have to experience if we accept his death as our own. For he has already borne in himself what we could never have borne and survived. He endured such hostility against himself because he was committed to our freedom from the power of sin.

When I consider just how unfair it might have been for God to have created that tree in Eden that caused so much grief and pain, I have only to look at the cross. How could he put that tree there? Because he had already determined that he would pay the greatest price for the stumbling block it would be for Adam and Eve. Even in giving us the freedom to trust him or trust ourselves, God already knew that he would suffer most for our choice. Somehow to him, the glory of fellowship with his created ones outweighed the price he would pay to set things right.

By enduring to the end, Jesus allowed sin to be fully conquered in him. Its spell over humanity was broken, and no longer does anyone have to be consumed by sin itself or God's wrath against it. The antidote not only worked in him, but it produced in his blood a fountain of life as well. Transfused into any person who desires it, his blood can cleanse us of sin and reunite us with God himself—fulfilling the dream that he had when he first decided to create man and woman and place them in the center of his creation.

"THIS CUP'S FOR YOU"

"This cup is the new covenant in my blood, which is poured out for you" (Luke 22:20).

Only a few hours before Jesus was arrested, as he shared a final meal with his disciples, Jesus spoke of the cup he would provide for us. Having drunk of the cup of wrath our sins deserved and having used that to condemn sin in sinful flesh, now he offers us a different cup. This cup is filled with his blood that has been purified and teems with life and grace.

Now he invites you to come and drink of his cup as the antidote that can cleanse not only the sins of your past, but the sin itself that wars in your heart and holds you captive to its desires. He has broken the bondage if you will only come and drink of him.

Unlike the Fall in Eden that subjected every one of us and the earth itself to the captivity of sin, this gift, freely given, must be freely received. God's desire for us to enter into relationship with him is still based on our choice.

Though he pursues us with an undying love and offers us to drink of the fountain of life, he will not make any of us come.

This is our choice, pure and simple.

The door is open; all we have to do is trust him enough to walk through it. There's that word again—trust! What Adam and Eve did not do in the Garden, we can now do through the work of the cross.

Enduring the antidote for sin was only part of it.

Something else happened on that cross that was meant to change our lives forever.

> *In him we have redemption through his blood, the forgiveness of sins, in accordance with the riches of God's grace that he lavished on us with all wisdom and understanding.*
>
> —EPHESIANS 1:7–8

For Your Personal Journey

Do you see God's wrath directed at sin or directed at you? It is one thing to say he loves the sinner and hates the sin, but sometimes we feel that he is out to get us as well. Wherever you see that in your thinking, ask God to help you change your mind and see things the way he does. He wants you to know that everything he has done in your life is intended to bring you into the fullness of his love. Where you don't understand that, ask him to show you.

For Group Discussion

1. Can you think of a time when your love for someone caused you to act on his or her behalf at great personal risk?

2. How does seeing God's wrath as the antidote for sin, rather than its punishment, affect your view of God and the cross?

3. Talk about the difference between the cup he drank and the cup he offers us to drink. How does that touch you?

4. Ask God to give each of you a personal revelation of the cross and confidence in all God accomplished there for you.

16

*You will trust God only as much
as you love him. And you will
love him not because you have
studied him; you will love him
because you have touched him—in
response to his touch. . . . Only if
you love will you make that final
leap into darkness. "Father, into
your hands I commend my spirit."*

Brennan Manning, *Lion and Lamb*

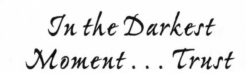

In the Darkest Moment . . . Trust

WHEN THE ENEMY DROVE A WEDGE between Eve and
her Creator, he had won the moment. Everything we do as a
result of not trusting God and his intentions toward us draws
us into the ever-deepening bondage of sin. That's as true of
indulging our selfish desires as it is of trying to appease him.

This is where an appeasement view of the cross serves us
so poorly. By viewing the cross as the offer of a get-out-of-
hell-free card rather than an invitation of friendship with
a gracious Father, we empty it of its power. By preying on

people's uncertainty about the afterlife, we can get them to go forward and pray a sinner's prayer or whatever else we ask them to do to ensure they go to heaven.

But then our problem only begins. Most go right back to living the way they had before, hopeful that they did enough not to worry about hell any longer. Some will get involved in a religious group or activity as an expression of their sincerity to God, but they all will soon discover that the reality of Christianity doesn't live up to its promise. They'll still find themselves overwhelmed by sin too great to conquer because they have not let him deal with the root of it.

For the power of the cross to significantly change our lives, it would have to restore the trust that was shattered in Eden.

And that it does in spectacular fashion.

FORSAKEN SON?

Perhaps Jesus' most puzzling words from the cross were in his cry of utter loneliness and despair: "My God, my God, why have you forsaken me?" Theologians have grappled with those words for centuries, trying to sort out what was happening between Father and Son at that moment.

Could the Faithful One be unfaithful to his Son at his darkest moment? Of course not. Even when Jesus told his disciples that they would all leave him alone, he said he would not be alone for the Father was with him. I don't believe for a minute that the Father forsook the Son. But there could be a vast difference here between what God *did* and what Jesus *perceived*. Jesus undoubtedly felt forsaken, but that doesn't mean he actually was.

Perhaps Psalm 22 holds a clue here since Jesus used the same words that David penned there. Read these excerpts from that psalm as David vacillates between his security in God's love and his fear that he had lost it:

- "My God, my God, why have you forsaken me? . . . Yet you are enthroned as the Holy One."

- "I cry out by day, but you do not answer. . . . [Yet] our fathers . . . trusted and you delivered them."

- "But I am a worm and not a man, scorned by men and despised by the people. . . . Yet you brought me out of the womb; you made me trust in you."

- "I am poured out like water, and all my bones are out of joint. . . . [Yet] he has not hidden his face from him but has listened to his cry for help."

David eloquently described the torrent of emotions that sin produces in us, overwhelming us with emptiness and making us feel abandoned. But he also affirmed that God is there nonetheless and in the end will have his way even through our agony.

When Jesus became sin for us, he entered into the full shame, darkness, and bondage of that sin. It is likely at the moment on the cross when God's wrath was consuming the sin he had become, he couldn't even see the Father with whom he had shared fellowship through all eternity. Sin blinded him, and he felt as if God had forsaken him. But that is the difference between the perception of sin and the reality of God.

We, too, feel abandoned by God at some of our darkest moments. It doesn't mean he's left us, only that we can't see him through the darkness. The resounding truth, however, is that God is always there, never turning his face against those who are his. To believe he did so with Christ is unthinkable.

That Jesus felt abandoned only shows the depth to which he experienced our sin. He entered into it fully, and for a brief time in eternity the Son knew what it was like to experience fatherlessness. How painful that must have been since he had lived every moment with his eye on his Father. He might even have lost sight of the purpose of the cross itself, so utterly dark was the depth of sin.

Unseen though he was, the Father was still there in the same measure that he had always been. But having become sin itself, Jesus could no longer sense his Father's presence. Perception would become its own reality as Jesus shared in the emptiness and loneliness that perhaps define hell itself. There is a mystery here far deeper than Scripture clarifies, and we must take care not to make more of it than we know. In allowing sin to touch the Godhead, a rift was created in the divine community. The price of our sin was borne in their wounding. How Jesus' cry must have ripped at his Father's heart, thinking himself the object of separation rather than love.

But the story didn't end there.

OUT OF THE DEPTHS

It was not long after his cry of abandonment that he offered the greatest demonstration of trust in the history of the world.

"Father, into your hands I commit my spirit."

To the Father he could not see.

To fulfill a plan that had long since faded from view.

In the utter despair and loneliness of the gut-wrenching agony of the cross, Jesus did what Adam and Eve could not do while living in the most pristine and beautiful of gardens.

He trusted his Father.

He committed his entire being into his Father's hands and in doing so breathed his last. The horror of the cross had reached its end. Sin had been consumed and his body spent. But his dying breath affirmed a heart of trust beyond comprehension. Now death's barrier had been crossed in a state of absolute trust and surrender. The power of death would be conquered, too.

Paul affirmmed repeatedly that God's work at the cross stands as the undeniable proof that we are loved. That God would go to such lengths to rescue us from our own wayward-ness so that we might be his friends forever secures God's motive concerning each of us. "Very rarely will anyone die for a righ-teous man. . . . But God demonstrates his own love for us in this: While we were still sinners, Christ died for us" (Rom. 5:7–8).

Whether it's the hen covering the chicks against the encroaching flames or the mother rushing into a bee swarm to scoop up her child, once love is demonstrated to that degree, how can it be doubted any longer? By inserting himself between us and our destruction, God wanted us to know that we could trust him through anything. When the reality of the cross sinks home, the enemy's wedge is dislodged.

No longer do we need to hesitate to trust this incredible Father and his intentions toward us, especially when we lose sight of what God is doing in our lives or question his seeming inactivity. Instead of doubting him, we can assume he's doing something greater than our expectations might allow and continue to walk with him instead of separating from him.

Not only does the cross demonstrate God's willingness to love us at the ultimate personal cost, but Jesus also modeled for us how we can live in that trust—"Into your hands I commit my spirit." When I can't figure out what God is doing; when I've just messed up to the greatest degree; when I'm lonely and empty, the answer is still the same: "Into your hands I commit my spirit."

THE FAITH OF JESUS

The heritage of the cross is a life lived in trust. It frees us from the bondage of sin that makes us feel estranged from his love and drives us to compensate for that, and provides for us the certainty that we are loved by the God of the universe. This is the faith he wants us to live by, and even that faith is his gift to us.

Few versions of the Bible translate Galatians 2:20 exactly as it appears in the original Greek. Paul wrote: "I have been crucified with Christ and I no longer live, but Christ lives in me. The life I live in the body, I live by *the* faith *of* the Son of God, who loved me and gave himself for me."

The vast majority translate it, "The life I live in the body, I live by faith *in* the Son of God." They could not conceive of what Paul might have meant by living by the faith *of* Jesus. So they translate it as "faith *in* the Son of God" since a number of other Scriptures talk about the importance of putting our faith in him. But Paul was talking about something different here. There is no ambiguity in the original language about the distinction between where our faith might be directed and to whom it belongs. It is clearly the latter. In other words, Paul was saying he lived off Jesus' faith, not by mustering up enough of his own.

Isn't that incredible? How often do you feel weak in faith? Try as hard as you might to believe, belief still escapes you. How do you muster up what you already lack? While they may be right, it is rarely helpful when people tell us we just need to trust Jesus more. Of course that's true, but how do we trust him more than we already do?

The answer lies here: Paul saw his life ending when Christ's ended at the cross. After that he didn't even live by his own human faith. He let Jesus live in him and let Jesus' trust in the Father stand for his.

My wife and I have done that as well. In the most severe trials of our journey, we have held each other in the storm, at times paralyzed by circumstances beyond our ability to endure. Sometimes with tearstained faces we have simply prayed, "Jesus, we choose to believe in the Father's love for us because you did. Give us your faith to stand right here in trust that our whole lives are in your hands."

It's amazing how that simple act works in us. It releases a power beyond our own abilities or intellect. Our eyes see a bit more clearly; our hearts find greater endurance. Answers we thought we needed no longer seem important. His presence and purpose alone prove sufficient in the storm. Eventually we come to recognize his hand doing something greater in our lives than we had hoped for at the time.

A LIFE LIVED IN TRUST

The apostle John told us that was the secret to living in this kingdom. He said he wrote his Gospel so that those who read it would "believe that Jesus is the Christ, the Son of God, and that by believing you may have life in his name" (John 20:31).

We have cheapened this verse with the popular notion that believing Jesus is the Christ is an affirmation of correct doctrine. If one gives mental assent to the fact that Jesus is the Christ then one has his life. That's not John's point. The word we translate "believe" is simply the verb form of "faith." Perhaps the word "trust" would bring out his fuller meaning.

John was not encouraging people to confess the right creed but inviting them to learn what God started to teach us in the Garden—how to trust him completely. John chose the events he reported from Jesus' life so that we might be stirred to trust who he is and by trusting every day, experience the life of God. We don't enter into this kingdom by a sinner's prayer, going forward at a religious gathering, or reciting an orthodox creed, but by learning to trust who he is and by living in that trust no matter what life hurls at us.

Those who learn and live in that trust discover God's life, even here in a broken and fallen world. What God accomplished in Christ on the cross not only defeated our sin but allows us to build a life of trust. He loves you absolutely and completely and will love you every day of your life on this planet and into the age to come.

The moment Jesus yielded to death on the cross, God's victory over sin and death was assured. What happened three days later only ratified the work he'd already finished. God raised him from the dead because he had already conquered it in his wholehearted trust in his Father and thus became the firstborn of a whole new race of men and women.

Now we can live as loved people, and he is alive to help us do it. No longer oppressed by the need to appease God, we are free to live in his love, and, as we'll see, that can completely transform everything about the way we think and live.

> *I have been crucified with Christ and I no longer live, but Christ lives in me. The life I live in the body, I live by the faith of the Son of God, who loved me and gave himself for me.*
> —GALATIANS 2:20 (AUTHOR'S TRANSL.)

For Your Personal Journey

Where is it easy for you to trust God, and where is it difficult? How can Jesus' example encourage you to trust God when he seems the most distant from you? Since it is his faith you want to live by, ask Jesus to teach you how he wants to grow your trust and how you can fix your hope on him in a way that runs deeper than your circumstances or feelings.

For Group Discussion

1. How would your life be different if you absolutely, completely trusted God for everything in your life?

2. Where does the darkness seem to surround you and make it difficult to understand what God is doing in you?

3. How can Jesus' actions on the cross provide the basis for you to learn how to trust Jesus through anything life can hurl at you?

4. Pray for one another that God will teach you in the everyday realities of your life what it is to trust that he is with you, working out his will in you.

SECTION IV

A Life
Lived in Love

*Christ's love compels us, because we are
convinced that one died for all, and therefore
all died. And he died for all, that those who live
should no longer live for themselves but for him
who died for them and was raised again.*

—2 Corinthians 5:14–15

17

God is not disillusioned with you, because he had no illusions about you in the first place.

GERALD COATES, UNPUBLISHED COMMENTS

Trying to Earn Points with Someone Who Is No Longer Keeping Score

FOR MY DEAR FRIEND, the words came with great pain. For me, they signaled an incredible breakthrough in my own relationship with God. The juxtaposition couldn't have been stranger.

In the previous few months he had watched his wife grow more distant and threaten to leave him. He had done everything he could to prove his love for her and to let her know that he would be willing to change anything to save their relationship.

But none of it had worked—not the new car he bought her, not the change in jobs she'd requested, not even his persistent words of entreaty. That morning she had left. He looked at me through teary eyes and said, "Wayne, I have come to realize that I have been trying to earn points with someone who was no longer keeping score."

In his situation I cannot imagine more painful words. My heart broke for him, and we spent the rest of our lunch together sorting out his options and finding out how I could support him in the difficult days ahead.

His words, however, had touched something far deeper and in a simple phrase had coalesced what the Father had been working into my life during the previous months. What had borne tragic news to him had signaled newfound freedom for me. I had spent all of my life in the faith doing with God what my friend had done with his wife. I, too, had been trying to earn points with someone who was no longer keeping score, though for far different reasons.

My friend's wife had stopped keeping score because she was no longer interested in saving their relationship. My Father had never kept score because he wanted nothing more than to cultivate a relationship with me. He had done that, not by throwing my scorecard away, but by completely filling it out himself.

That's what Paul meant when he said that Jesus died on the cross so that "the righteous requirements of the law might be fully met in us, who do not live according to the sinful nature but according to the Spirit" (Rom. 8:4). For someone who had lived many years imagining God as the divine Scorekeeper, this moment was a glorious epiphany.

God's not counting anymore, and that means I don't have to either!

NOT LESS LOVED BUT FULLY LOVED

If Adam and Eve's troubles began when they lost sight of how deeply God loved them, doesn't it stand to reason that our whole lives will change when we come to know the depth of his love for us? That's exactly what our Father wants the reality of the cross to produce in us.

In this final section, we will look at what it means to live every day in the confidence of his love for us. We'll discover that when we live in this reality, everything about our lives and our faith will take on different meaning and tap new motivations. Rather than providing an excuse for falling victim to sin, our security in his love will actually destroy the root of sin and show us how to live as his free people on the earth.

But let us be certain of the process at the outset. You cannot implement the practical implications as an attempt to become secure in his love. That is backward, confusing the cause with the results. It will only produce another form of legalism—trying to earn by effort what God has made a gift.

Freedom to grow in him comes when you recognize that his love for you isn't affected by your actions. In *What's So Amazing About Grace?*, Philip Yancey said it as clearly as we need to understand it: "Grace means there is nothing we can do to make God love us more . . . and there is nothing we can do to make God love us less. God already loves us as much as an infinite God can possibly love."

Our only choice is whether or not to *live* loved, trusting that his eye is on us and that he can work out in us everything he desires. That is the challenge of life in God's kingdom. He has done everything to demonstrate his irrefutable love, but he will not make us live there. We can still live less loved, pursuing our own agenda with our own resources and in the process not only destroying ourselves but hurting others as well.

The choice is yours, and it can't be made once for a lifetime. This choice is made every day in every circumstance in which you find yourself. Do you trust that he loves you even in this, or will you fall back on your own wisdom and desires?

NOT RELIGION, BUT RELATIONSHIP

There are two ways to hide from God's love—rebellion and religion. Rebellion, illustrated in the prodigal son, defies God's love and seeks to cover up guilt and shame through the indulgence of sensual desires. Religion, on the other hand, is far more subtle. It seeks its cover-up through good works and obligation. However, like the prodigal's older brother, it still denies the Father's place in our lives and leads us no closer to knowing him for who he really is.

Simply, religion is keeping score—striving for acceptance through our own performance whether it be in our good works or in ritualistic activities. Those things put the focus squarely on us and what we can do to be accepted by God, thereby dooming us to failure.

Most of Paul's letters were written because even the earliest believers found themselves trading relationship for religion. Instead of learning to live in the security of his love, they would go back to the traditions, creeds, disciplines, and laws as an attempt to earn it themselves. He reminded them again and again that God's love would take them further than their own efforts and achievements ever would. But his words often fell on deaf ears then, as they have in generations since.

Why do so many enjoy striving for God's acceptance, even after he went to such lengths to prove it was already ours? Perhaps they feel more secure if they think they can control the relationship. Perhaps they're afraid that if they no longer have to earn his acceptance, they'll find themselves using grace as an excuse to pursue their selfish desires. Perhaps they don't want a relationship with him at all; they simply want his help when they hurt and the coveted get-out-of-hell-free card.

Religion offers us the illusion of earning acceptance, but it is only a cheap substitute for the reality of life in him. God's desire is to engage us in a life-changing relationship. He knew the "life-changing" would come only out of the relationship. Thus he demonstrated his love for us before we did anything to make ourselves worthy of it. By doing so, he wanted us to stop trying to earn it and just live in light of it.

What would you do today if you knew God absolutely loved you? God knows the answer to that question will lead you further into his life than the strivings of religion ever can. The key to living a productive Christian life is not waking up every day trying to be loved by God, but waking up in the awareness that you are already his beloved.

NOT A FORMULA, BUT A FRIENDSHIP

By releasing us from the terrible burden of trying to earn his friendship, God put the focus right where he wanted it—on the relationship he always wanted to have with each of us. He wants to be a closer friend than any other we've ever had: to share our joys, our pains, even our failures as he teaches us how to live in him.

Daily, God wants us to discover more about him and how he wants to be involved with us. This is an intensely personal process. Try as we might to standardize that relationship by offering a checklist of actions necessary to cultivate it, we will always fall short. No living relationship thrives through the use of a checklist because it is far more dynamic than any list can facilitate. God can be personal enough to develop this friendship with each of us as we invite him to do so.

Some people have asked me if this kind of friendship risks trivializing God and reduces our awe of him. I have not found that to be so. Those who treat God as a buddy who thinks and acts just as they do always make me wonder if it's the living God they've found or an illusion of their own minds. God is who he is. He is the almighty, holy God who created the heavens and the earth. He is more magnificent than we can ever conceive. I can approach him only with confidence because that's the way he wanted it, but that doesn't diminish in my mind for one moment who he is.

Some have argued that if we wouldn't be so casual with an earthly sovereign, why would we presume to do so with God Almighty? I know what they mean. If I had the opportunity to meet a president or a king, I would dress up in my finest and extend to that person all the decorum the station demanded. But it would be impossible to become friends in that environment, wouldn't it?

Does the king or president want that with everyone? I wouldn't think so. What persons can go to the president in their comfortable clothes, jump up into his lap, and laugh and play with him? His children, of course. That's what God has offered us—not the relationship of a subject, but that of a son or daughter who can know him as he really is and not be intimidated by that. He didn't want to use his magnificence to dwarf us, but to elevate us into a friendship with an incredible Father. That could never make him less awesome, only more so.

NOT FOR HIM, BUT WITH HIM

As you grow increasingly certain that his love for you is not connected to your performance, you will find yourself released from the horrible burden of doing something for him. You'll realize that your greatest ideas and most passionate deeds will fall far short of what he really wants to do through you.

I used to be driven to do something great for God. I volunteered for numerous opportunities and worked hard in the hopes that some book I was writing, some church I was planting, or some organization I was helping would accomplish great things for God. While I think God used my misguided zeal in spite of myself, nothing I did ever rose to the level of my expectations. Instead, my pursuits seemed to distract me from God, consume my life, and leave me stressed out or worn out.

I'm not driven anymore. I haven't tried to do anything great for God in more than a decade, and yet I have seen him use my life in ways that always exceed my expectations. What changed? I did, by his grace.

My desire to do something great for God served me far more than it ever did him. It kept me too busy to enjoy him and distracted me from the real ministry opportunities he brought across my path every day.

I used to start my day laying out my plans before God and seeking his blessing on them. How silly! Why would I want God to be the servant of my agenda? God's plans for my day far exceed mine. I can almost hear him now as I awaken: "Wayne, I'm going to touch some people today. Do you want to come along?"

It's amazing how gentle that is, but all the more powerful because it is. I don't have to go. God's work won't be thwarted by my lack of participation. He will touch people anyway, but I wouldn't miss it for the world. He does things I've never dreamed of and uses me in ways I could never conceive. His focus on touching people instead of managing programs has revolutionized my view of ministry. It requires no less diligence on my part but directs that diligence in far more fruitful endeavors.

If you've never known the joy of simply living in God's acceptance instead of trying to earn it, your most exciting days in Christ are ahead of you. People who learn to live out of a genuine love relationship with the God of the universe will live in more power, more joy, and more righteousness than anyone motivated by fear of his judgment.

> *All this is from God, who reconciled us to himself through Christ and gave us the ministry of reconciliation: that God was reconciling the world to himself in Christ, not counting men's sins against them.*
> —2 CORINTHIANS 5:18–19

For Your Personal Journey

Spend a few moments thinking what you are still counting in your relationship with God. Is it failures? Minutes in prayer? Number of converts? If you find yourself doing those things, ask God to help you receive what he has already given you. Stop doing anything that seeks to earn his love and learn to do what you do simply because you already have his love. This is quite a change of mind that only God's Spirit can produce.

For Group Discussion

1. What kinds of things do you count to determine your status with God?

2. When you feel as if you're not doing enough for God, what do you usually focus on?

3. Have you tried to do some great thing for God? How did it turn out? Did he use it to touch some lives anyway? (Isn't he amazing?)

4. What would you do tomorrow if you absolutely knew God loved you and just wanted to share your life?

5. What barrier(s) do you see in your life that makes it difficult for you to accept God's love for you? Pray together that God will show you how to get past the barrier.

*Never let us be discouraged
with ourselves; it is not when
we are conscious of our faults
that we are the most wicked:
on the contrary, we are less
so. We see by a brighter light.
And let us remember, for our
consolation, that we never
perceive our sins till he begins
to cure them.*

FRANCOIS FÉNELON (1651–1715)

So Sin Isn't Important to God?

THE PASTOR INVITED ME TO SPEAK to a retreat of
his elders. "Would you teach us about grace? Our leaders
really need it!"

On Friday night I began to lay the foundation for an
understanding of God's grace. They were not impressed.
They didn't laugh at my stories or respond to my overtures.
They were either suspicious of me or hostile to the material, I couldn't tell which. I hoped for better in the morning,
but the mood hadn't changed at all.

After a few more moments of unsuccessfully trying to win them over, I finally stopped. "Let me ask you a question," I began. "Am I making any sense at all?"

Eyes darted around the room uncomfortably, but most settled on an elderly gentleman in the corner. After a moment, he spoke. "What I hear you saying is that these young people coming to our church don't need to jump through the same hoops I've been forcing myself through all my life."

Good, they have got it! I thought. I nodded as he paused.

"Well, I'll tell you something." The mood got darker. "If you think I'm going to let them get away with that, you're a bigger fool than I give you credit for!" I glanced around the room and saw nods of agreement. Obviously I was in the minority.

"So why am I here?" I said, turning to the pastor.

"I told you, we don't understand grace!"

And they didn't. Their security with God was derived from their rules and rituals. Through them they had staked out the high ground above the rest of the people and were not about to give it up. They made serving God their god and missed knowing the living God.

"BUT" THEOLOGY

I understood their dilemma because I had lived there, too. Who hasn't seen people use God's grace as an excuse to guiltlessly chase their own agenda? They accept God's forgiveness and an eternity in heaven but go on living in the same captivity as the world around them. Not wanting to apportion "cheap grace" to people who don't want to do things God's way, we find ourselves constructing a list of expectations to help define what a true Christian does.

It's as if we can keep the message of grace intact only for the first fifteen minutes of someone's birth into God's kingdom. After that we start loading them down with the obligations of being a good Christian: "Of course we are saved by grace, *but* that doesn't mean we can just sit around and do nothing. God is a loving Father, *but* don't take advantage of that because he is also a severe Judge. We are not saved by our works, *but* we still need to live lives that please him." The latter usually consists of some mix of Bible reading, prayer, church attendance, and righteous deeds.

By embracing this "but" theology, we end up right where we began, with a performance-based relationship with God. We have to live every day concerned about whether we have done enough to be good Christians and judge others around us with the same standards. This takes away not only the joy of knowing God, but also the encouragement of our relationships with one another.

Whenever we add anything to God's work on the cross, the message is distorted and we rob it of its power. Paul made it clear that the cross alone had totally transformed him: "May I never boast except in the cross of our Lord Jesus Christ, through which the world has been crucified to me, and I to the world" (Gal. 6:14).

Grace doesn't need any add-ons. Even though Paul watched people who used their newfound freedom as an excuse for the flesh and warned them not to do so, he knew he could never change them by adding human effort to God's grace. He knew the fix lay elsewhere.

It is as paradoxical a truth as Jesus' warning that we save our lives by losing them: living in his grace leads to freedom from sin; living in his judgment leads to even greater sin. It has always been so, though it defies human logic. That's because we are far more used to being conformed by external pressures than we are to being transformed by his inner presence. Many, having never experienced the latter, doubt it will even work.

But it does. Once you experience God's delight over you as his child and the joy of friendship that produces, you will find yourself abandoning your own desires and embracing his. Of course that delight doesn't mean he affirms everything you do. He simply knows that without him you are powerless against sin and that whatever strength of will you can conjure up will last only a few months before fading into a deeper bondage.

So God still cares about sin—deeply! Sin destroys what he loves. He wants to change you by teaching you how to live loved every day. When you learn to recognize his voice in your ear and his hand in your life, you will want to be even more like him.

THE CONSEQUENCES OF SIN

We make a fatal mistake when we try to force Scripture to offer redemption to those who want to go to heaven but who do not want a relationship with the living God. By trying to offer some minimal standard of conduct that will allow them to qualify for salvation while continuing to pursue their own agendas, we distort the gospel and destroy its power, and we concoct legalistic games to give them a false sense of security.

In fact, the New Testament has nothing to say to people who want God's salvation without wanting *him*. The Scriptures are an unabashed invitation to live as a child of the most incredible Father in the universe. As you do, you will yearn to be like him. You will discover that God's way is better than anything you can imagine, and you'll lay down your agenda to embrace his.

Grace doesn't mitigate all the consequences of sin. Certainly it allows God to forgive us so that our relationship with him is unimpeded by our failures, and it does negate the culmination of sin in spiritual death. But grace doesn't cancel out the temporal consequences of sin.

If I vent my anger on my children, grace doesn't stop the damage it does to them or what it destroys in me. The person who engages in immoral behavior may still get pregnant or contract a fatal disease. If you take advantage of people for your own gain, they still experience the loss or the pain. A murderer's victim is still dead.

Viewed this way, sin is its own punishment. I used to look at sin with longing, seeing it as a forbidden pleasure God denied me to prove my sincerity. I could look at those who seemed to get away with it in envy because I could not.

But sin diminishes who God really made us to be. Putting our wisdom and desires above his distorts who we really are and leaves a wake of hurt people behind us.

No one who understands the Father's grace will think it lets us get away with sin. Rather, it allows us to see our weaknesses and failures in the full light of God's love. It encourages us to invite the Father into the darkest places of our hearts and ask him to change us.

That's why I'm suspicious of those who think repentance undoes the consequences of their sin and that people should just forgive and forget. True repentance doesn't deny the pain we've caused others but owns up to it. Forgiveness isn't a covering for sin, but reason to be honest with our faults and seek to rectify whatever damage our sins have caused others.

GRACE WITH A PURPOSE

Those who distort grace do so because they see it only as a ticket to heaven. If the reason Jesus died on the cross was to save us from hell, then how do we get people to live the Christian life?

Such thinking misses the greater point. God did not extend his grace to us merely to forgive our sins and let us into heaven. Those are secondary benefits, not the primary objective. The purpose of grace is to grant us access into his presence every day. Grace qualifies us for the relationship we could never earn on our merits.

This grace doesn't let us get away with sin, but in fact "it teaches us to say 'No' to ungodliness and worldly passions" (Titus 2:12).

God knows that as we grow in friendship with him and discover how to trust the fact that he loves us completely, the root of sin will be destroyed. Grace doesn't diminish God's desire for our holiness but clarifies the process. Righteousness doesn't produce relationship. Relationship produces righteousness.

That's why Paul despised the righteousness that came from human effort. He had sampled it for most of his life. He knew it was merely an illusion of outward performance that would constantly frustrate its pursuer. Like Adam and Eve's choice to trust themselves over their Creator, it would lead to utter failure.

But when God revealed his grace to Paul and he discovered the love Father held in his eye for him, even after the atrocities that he had committed, Paul was changed. Knowing he deserved death and had been spared meant his life no longer belonged to him. The true treasure lies in knowing God in his fullness and the Son whom he raised from the dead.

The power of the cross had opened an eternal friendship between himself and the Father. As he learned to trust that love, Paul watched his life change. Appetites of the flesh waned and he found himself acting in ways that surprised him so much, he dared not take credit for them.

He referred to his new behavior as the righteousness that comes from trusting God and knew it was the exact opposite of the righteousness that works had produced in him. Once he tasted of the lifestyle that trust produced, he never wanted to return to his old ways.

Living in the transformation that trust produces is the real deal. When you watch yourself speak a kind word where anger would have surfaced before, or find yourself uninterested in something that used to drive you mad with desire, or sacrifice something you hold dear without hardly a second thought, then you will know what Paul knew.

It's righteousness as only God can produce. Taste it once, and you'll never be satisfied with anything less.

> *. . . That I may gain Christ and be found in him, not having a righteousness of my own that comes from the law, but that which is through faith in Christ—the righteousness that comes from God and is by faith.*
> —PHILIPPIANS 3:8–9

For Your Personal Journey

Has a false notion of grace diminished your passion for righteousness, or has it made you hungrier for the righteousness that comes from trusting God? If the former, ask God to draw you closer to him so that your love for him will produce a desire to be like him. Also, look for ways that you put righteousness before relationship, thinking that your performance makes you more acceptable to God. Ask him to teach you what it means to trust him in the pressing details of your life right now.

For Group Discussion

1. Talk about grace as you understood it in the past in contrast to what you read in this chapter.

2. What add-ons to grace have you tried? Did they work?

3. How do you find yourself viewing sin—as a forbidden pleasure or a destroying presence?

4. Share an incident where you experienced righteousness that grew naturally out of simply learning to trust God instead of leaning on yourself.

5. Where do you see yourself putting the demands of righteousness before the joys of relationship? Pray that God will help you reverse this process and learn to delight in him.

19

Once God is known as Father all methods to attain to security, prosperity and assurance in the world are exposed as useless enslavement. If one knows God as Father then there is security about everything.

DAVID BOAN AND JOHN YATES,
UNPUBLISHED MANUSCRIPT

A Lifetime of Learning to Trust

THE MECHANIC HAD ESTIMATED the repair to my car heater at well over three hundred dollars. Imagine my shock, then, when I went to pick it up and he said, "That will be $18.75."

I looked at him, uncertain of what I'd heard, and he simply smiled back. I repeated his price in surprise. "What happened?"

"It wasn't what we thought. We found a loose connection and tightened it for you."

Being mechanically challenged and having seen too many *60 Minutes* reports on unscrupulous mechanics, I expect them all to cheat me. I've taken my car in too many times for a thirty-dollar oil change and come out with four hundred dollars' worth of repairs I was never sure I needed. It had never worked the other way around.

This was my first visit to that mechanic, but it certainly was not my last. By demonstrating his integrity when he could have easily taken advantage of me, he gained my trust. I went away assured that I had finally found an honest mechanic, and as long as we lived in that community he was the only mechanic I allowed to touch my cars.

One simple act of integrity secured my trust in his workmanship, and he never disappointed me.

God wanted to secure our trust the same way but on a far larger scale. By taking our sin into himself and destroying it at the cost of his own life, he showed us the lengths to which his love would go for us. That act provided a source of trust for us as constant as he is. Never again would we doubt his intentions toward us no matter what happened.

TO TRUST OR NOT TO TRUST?

Most of our lessons in trust have been incredibly painful. Haven't we all been disappointed by people we thought would treat us fairly or compassionately? Perhaps you've experienced the betrayal of people you considered close friends simply because you no longer served their needs or desires.

Through the course of life we learn to keep a wary eye on people, knowing how few trustworthy people there really are. That may sound jaded, but Jesus lived that way, too. He didn't entrust himself to anyone because he knew what was inside people (see John 2:24). So of course our attempts to trust others will often be frustrated, but that's because God never wanted us to trust others. He wanted us to love others but to trust him alone.

But learning to trust him can also be a struggle. In my spiritual journey I've often been disillusioned by trusting God. It seems so easy when all our circumstances are pleasant, but when painful and desperate circumstances come crashing down on us, he sometimes seems to ignore our most ardent prayers. Who hasn't trusted God to do something, then watched him seemingly fail? How do those moments help us learn to trust?

Interestingly enough, they do! I used to think that being disillusioned with God was sinful, but I have since learned it is a valuable part of the process. Being disillusioned with God means I have illusions about him that need to be "dissed." The fact is he has never failed to love me completely, despite how it may have appeared. He didn't do what I expected, not because he loved me less as I feared, but because his way of resolving my need exceeded my own. "Immeasurably more than all we ask or imagine," is how Paul phrased it (Eph. 3:20).

Looking back, I thought I could trust God to make my life easy, to provide what I wanted and steer me clear of any painful experiences. That wasn't God's agenda for me at all. He wanted to imprint his glory into my life, to make me a man who would bear his image to a fallen world. So he rarely dealt with circumstances the way I wanted, and by not accepting the way in which he was loving me, my confidence was eroded. As long as our trust in him is based on circumstances (and our misinterpretation of them), it will shift as often as the winds.

Through the cross God provided a way for us to trust him that would transcend our own preferences and intellect, a way that is able to take us through the darkest circumstances, not doubting his love, but resting in it.

LEARNING THE LANGUAGE OF GOD

Several years ago I traveled around France for a month while on a speaking tour. Often I stayed in homes where no one was able to speak English. I found it frustrating to live so near some of God's treasures without the language to understand their stories.

I have felt like that in my journey with God as well. Often I have no idea what he's trying to say to me or what he's trying to do in my life. I am more comfortable with the language of human effort and anxiety than I am the language of trust. But this is one treasure I'm not going to miss, no matter how hard it is for me to learn.

Trusting the Father's love for you simply means that every day, in every circumstance, you can rest assured God knows who you are, cares more deeply about you than you do yourself, and is capable of working out his glory in you.

When you trust him, you will find yourself cooperating with his work going on in you and around you. Trust is not coasting through life assuming that whatever happens must be God's will. Rather it is an active partnership that rises out of your relationship with him. Without that, what many call trust is simply a Christian version of fatalism or complacency.

Whenever I talk about trust, this question invariably arises: "Does that mean I just do nothing and God will do it all?" We are so schooled in trusting our own efforts that we can't see anything beyond that. We equate trusting him with doing nothing because we know that most of what we do is driven by the fact that we don't think he's doing anything at all.

Trusting God doesn't lead to lethargy or provide an excuse to be slothful. Those who are learning to trust God will discover how to actively participate with him in the work he is doing. Even though Paul warned us against trusting our own efforts, he showed us that cooperating with him can be costly. "To this end I labor, struggling with all his energy, which so powerfully works in me" (Col. 1:29).

The difference is striking. For many years I thought I knew what God wanted with my life and pursued it with a passion. Others encouraged me, thinking it was what God wanted, too.

Most of that agenda, however, was motivated by my own insecurities and need to be successful. No matter how I dressed that up by calling it God's promise, or thinking that my success would benefit the kingdom of God, he did not help me pursue my own agenda.

Trying to make it happen on my own led to frustration and burnout. As I've grown to trust him more and see more clearly what he wants to accomplish in and through my life, I find myself even more willing to go the extra mile in what he asks me to do. When I'm on his agenda, I find, like Paul, that it taps a deeper reserve than mere human effort. It allows me to draw from his strength, which does not burn me out.

When Jesus asked people to "repent and believe" the gospel, he was not asking them to be sorry for their sins and embrace an orthodox theology. He was asking them to forfeit their own agenda and embrace his. That's the invitation to the kingdom. It is not whether we want to go to heaven or hell, but whether we want to trust God or continue trusting ourselves.

To do that he will teach us how to recognize his presence with us. He will teach us how to understand his heart and how to confidently follow his will. But the curriculum for that is not where you might first expect it.

LIFE AT THE END OF YOUR ROPE

Jesus seemed to think backward about everything. "You're blessed when you're at the end of your rope. With less of you there is more of God and his rule." That's how Eugene Peterson translates the first beatitude in *The Message,* and I think he gets to the heart of it.

I've never heard anyone stand up during testimony time and say, "I know I'm really blessed today because I'm all out of options. I've lost everything and am at the end of my rope with nothing left to hold on to." We don't think of such people as blessed. We think of them as needy. We consider ourselves blessed when all our needs are met and there are no dark clouds on the horizon. But we are wrong!

Every New Testament writer echoes Jesus' words. All of them tell us that we can rejoice in our most difficult moments because Jesus will be working things out in those seasons that we would never let him touch when all is well. He didn't tell us to rejoice for the bad times, but *in them* because he would convert our pain into his glory.

The truth is we grow in trust only at moments of extremity. If we can do it ourselves, we will! If we're sure we can fix things, we won't listen for him. If we have enough money, time, energy, talent—or know others who do—we'll try that first.

Taking us to the end of our rope is really taking us to the end of ourselves. That's why he calls us "blessed" at those moments. While I appreciate the seasons of rest and refreshing God brings into my life, I realize that only by facing my own inadequacies and the foolishness of my own desires can I really experience the glory of God's kingdom. We don't come easily to those moments, but when we finally give up trying to save ourselves, that's where we taste of his immeasurable glory.

Along this journey you will notice that every good thing he has imprinted in your heart came at your most difficult moments. I don't think for a moment that God orchestrates these times, because the consequences of living in a fallen world will provide ample opportunities. What amazes me is how he uses the most hurtful moments for his purpose. You'll even see him use what others intend for evil to purify your heart and teach you to depend on him even more.

Much of the curriculum for this journey lies in the very circumstances you're begging God to change. This journey is at once more painful than you can imagine and filled with more wonder than you can contain. Don't think it a broad road, for it is not. You'll find even your dearest friends in Christ may not understand the most difficult places in your journey. But trust him to take you through them and he will. In doing so he will make you a little more like him.

I don't know that we'll ever get comfortable at the end of the rope, but at least we don't have to dread it or think it proof he has abandoned us.

BEYOND YOUR FAILURES

A friend of mine recently lost his job and is actively seeking another. One morning he told me that a plum job had just escaped his grasp and that someone far less qualified got it.

Knowing my friend's desire to live in God's life, I asked him if he thought anything could have prevented him from getting that job if God wanted it for him. "If I messed up somehow," he responded.

"So are you saying that you believe God isn't bigger than your mistakes?"

It's a misconception far too many of us indulge. If our freedom to trust God hinges on our ability to get everything right, then we're really back to trusting ourselves, aren't we? If God isn't bigger than our halting attempts to learn how to walk with him, we might as well give up now.

But he is! That's the lesson he taught Peter on the night he let him face the biggest failure of his life. He told him it would happen, but Peter was certain that he was strong enough to endure any threat to his relationship with Jesus.

Don't you wish Jesus had just sent Peter home, telling him to lock the doors, crawl under the covers, and wait for Sunday morning? Jesus didn't even try to stop Peter from following him to Caiaphas's house where he would betray his friend.

What's even more amazing is that before Peter's failure Jesus had already prayed him past it. "I have prayed for you, . . . that your faith may not fail. And when you have turned back, strengthen your brothers"(Luke 22:32). Please understand what Jesus was doing here. He had already factored Peter's failure in before he had even committed it. He knew what Peter didn't know. He could have saved him the anguish, but he wanted Peter to come to the end of his rope and learn that he could not trust in his own ability to follow Jesus.

I suspect it was the most painful but most joyous lesson Peter ever learned. Where there was less of Peter, there was more of God and his rule. Don't think for a moment that the slips and spills of learning to live in the Father's love will exclude you from his table. God is able to work in you and through you despite what you lack.

He knows that learning to live in the confidence of his love amid the realities of everyday life is the most difficult thing you'll ever learn.

A JOURNEY FOR A LIFETIME

One of my friends was shackled by perfectionism. Whenever we talked about grace, he wanted to believe it, but was always so aware of his shortcomings that he couldn't bring himself to trust God until he performed better.

But one day God used a hobby of his to teach him about grace. He loves to work with wood and to make decorations for his home. The light dawned for him when he noticed how differently he and his wife view his hobby. She loves the finished product and delights in displaying it in their home. He, however, enjoys the process of making it far more. He loves to take a raw piece of wood and fashion it. Once it's finished he is already on to what he wants to do next. "I finally realized that God not only wants the product, but he actually enjoys the process."

He's right. God enjoys taking fearful slaves to sin and teaching them how to live as beloved sons and daughters. He knows how to peel off layers of selfishness and shame to shape his image in us.

That's why the writer of Hebrews called Jesus the Author and Perfecter of our faith. He initiated it on the cross, and with painstaking care he continues to carve, sand, and buff until we become the treasure he fashioned in his heart at the beginning of time.

It's a process he controls from start to finish, and it's a journey that will last a lifetime. You can't make it happen, but you can choose to cooperate with him and embrace the incredible process he'll use to produce his glory in you.

> *Let us fix our eyes on Jesus, the author and perfecter*
> *of our faith, who for the joy set before him endured*
> *the cross, scorning its shame, and sat down at the*
> *right hand of the throne of God.*
> —HEBREWS 12:2

<><><><><><><><><><><>

For Your Personal Journey

Where are you being stretched to the end of your rope? Where is God exposing the weaknesses of your own strength and the foolishness of your best wisdom? Give up the idea that your failures have brought you to this moment, for it is an incredible work of God calling you to trust him more than you have in the past. Ask God to teach you how to give up self-sufficiency and learn to trust him. Then do whatever it is that trusting God's love would lead you to do and learn to ignore the ravings of your anxieties and fears.

For Group Discussion

1. Share some experiences of how the Father has taught you to trust him when you've been at the end of your rope.

2. Read Romans 8:31–32 and discuss how the cross guarantees that the Father loves you today in the midst of whatever circumstances you are facing.

3. Even though the advice "You just need to trust God more" is true, why is it the worst possible advice to give someone in the midst of a crisis?

4. Explore why we seem to be able to support people only when we understand what they are going through. How can we support people on their journey even though God is doing things in their lives that we don't understand?

5. Ask God together to teach you how to walk out this trust in the everyday circumstances of your lives.

20

(When you) become totally depen-
dent upon the life of Christ . . .
(you will never be) so released at
last from the self distrust which
has made you at one moment an
arrogant loud-mouthed braggart,
and the next moment the victim
of your own self-pity—and either
way, always in bondage to the fear
of other men's opinions.

MAJOR IAN THOMAS, THE SAVING
LIFE OF CHRIST

Shamelessly Free

IT CAN WEAR SO MANY DISGUISES so well it's not always easy to recognize.

It will help you boast at your achievements and contrive excuses for your mistakes.

It can turn a simple gift of God into feelings of superiority and then at the first sign of trouble plunge you to the depths of inferiority.

It can take you captive through the compliments of others and make you feel rejected by the most genuine criticism.

It can make you rabidly chase an illusion of success that never satisfies and completely paralyzes you with a fear of failure.

It will let you take credit for good things you don't deserve and blame others for their hard times.

One minute it can make you smug in self-righteousness and the next overwhelm you with guilt and self-loathing.

Shame is the unfortunate inheritance of humanity's captivity in sin. You were born with it whispering in your ear. Until you find freedom from it in the Father's love, shame will, like a spreading cancer, sink its tentacles into everything you think or do.

What a horrible burden it is to measure our worth by everything we do and every word spoken about us. As long as you listen to shame, it will devour your energy and leave you with a distorted perspective of God's work in you and those around you. Since the day Adam covered up for shame with those itchy fig leaves, we have been at our worst when following its counsel or trying to hide its presence.

But when you find your security in the awesome love of God, its voice is unmasked. No longer do you have to play its games by worrying about what others think. Then you'll really know what it is to live as God's child in the earth.

A TOUCHDOWN FOR JESUS

He was a high-priced cornerback playing for a professional football team, suffering from an overdose of media scrutiny. Having sold his talents as a free agent, his subsequent performance had been disappointing. People were saying he was overpriced and overrated. Twice that evening he had been beaten for touchdowns and knew the media would have a field day with his poor performance. But a few minutes into overtime he intercepted a pass and ran it back for the winning touchdown.

As the Monday night telecast went off the air, a microphone was shoved into the celebration. Through an irrepressible, mile-wide grin he yelled, "I just thank the Lord Jesus for giving me the chance to prove myself. I felt like he was saying that I had the faith to make this happen."

While he celebrated his touchdown, I grieved for his theology. He seemed to unmask his own shame by boasting that his touchdown validated his faith. Can you imagine what he lives with every day if he links his trust in God to his performance on a football field?

I sometimes cringe when professional athletes talk about God. What comes out often paints God as a success deity, rewarding the faithful with victory. One of those I respect the most said his Super Bowl victory vindicated his obedience to play for a certain team. What about the men God had called to the city who lost the Super Bowl? Was their obedience less significant or their lives less valuable to God?

Other athletes have said that God rewards with victories those who will give him the most glory. Is that why we see people kneel down in the end zone and acknowledge God after a touchdown but get angry when they miss a tackle or throw an interception?

You can't blame them, really. To get to the highest echelon of athletic competition, these men and women have learned to live on the success of their performance. They've been trained to measure their value by it because that's how everyone else around them measures it. They've obviously had a lot of success to get to that level of competition. But it can result in some greatly distorted values.

Watch a championship game or a match and you'll notice that the highs of winning are just too high, the lows too low. Rather than championships, perhaps they could be called "pageants to manic-depression." No moderate ground exists here. John Madden, the revered football analyst, said this of professional sports: "The highs of winning never equal the lows of losing." Even coming out second best in all the world seemingly forces a team to slink off in shame and suffer months of embarrassment. Even fans take on the same attitudes of superiority or shame.

Please don't read this as an indictment against professional athletes, because we all do it. It's just that most of our best or our worst moments aren't on television.

SHAME-BASED LIVING

We have all felt the pervasive power of shame when we've been embarrassed by something we've done or something someone else has said. Our faces flush and our stomachs grind, and we want to dig a hole and crawl into it. But it also works much deeper than that.

Shame tells us that people could never love us if they really knew what we had been part of in the past or knew the temptations, doubts, and motives that still lurk beneath the surface. Aren't there things you hope no one ever finds out about you?

So we pretend to be whatever we think will make us feel included and don't realize that everyone else is doing it, too. When people ask for my help to deal with a sin or struggle, they almost always preface their confession with a disclaimer. "I know probably no one else is dealing with this, but. . . ." Shame often keeps us from being authentic enough to realize that others are struggling with the same things.

Feeling inferior is only one side of shame. Those who act superior and boast of their accomplishments also are reacting to shame. Those behaviors only act as a cover for a deep sense of personal inadequacy, usually at other people's expense.

All of this shame makes us easy to manipulate. Our desire to be liked, to fit in, and to not be embarrassed is what the world uses to press us into its mold, and also what we often use in reverse to get what we want from others. Most advertising appeals to these motives at some level.

Organized religion can also be a master of its use. When people want us to do something for them, they will press on these self-needs as a way to make us respond. Shame makes it impossible for us to say no and gives power to gossip. It threatens us with humiliation or with being left out if we don't conform to what others want, and it promises approval and affirmation when we obey.

We learn this pattern early. Children are often made to feel that they are loved and appreciated to the degree that they can meet their parents' expectations. It's ironic that parents are so mystified about the effects of peer pressure when their children start caring more about what their friends think of them than what their parents do. It's because of the same use of shame.

The fear of "what others might think" can both restrain us from doing what we know is right and entice us to do what ultimately harms us.

I remember receiving a gold-plated pin when I was eleven years old for two years of unbroken attendance at Sunday school. The affirmation I received for my accomplishment and the applause of all the adults in the congregation was an intoxicating brew. It made me feel superior to others who had not been so dedicated and helped launch me on a persistent quest to drink of that well for most of my spiritual journey.

I thought that thirst was my friend, beckoning me closer to Jesus, not realizing for almost thirty years it was my jailer, pushing me to serve other people's expectations. Jesus didn't want to use my shame to spur me to greater things, he wanted to set me free from it.

SHAME-FREE LIVING

This story has always amazed me. A woman whose reputation for sin was well known in her community walked into the home of a Pharisee while a group of them were sharing a meal with Jesus. She made her way around the table until she found him, then she poured expensive perfume over his feet and wiped them with her hair.

How could she even go into a home of those who despised her so much? And how could she touch Jesus that way when surely everyone in the room would misinterpret her act of love? Shouldn't she have been too ashamed to even show her face there? You would think so, but no! Obviously she had been deeply touched by Jesus, her sins had been forgiven, and now the only thing that mattered to her in that room full of disparaging looks was the look of appreciation she saw in his eyes.

What began in the Garden—our utter sense of shame—is swallowed up in the presence of Jesus. She was liberated from the oppressive need of worrying about what others thought of her and was able to simply do what she wanted to do most. Discovering how much the Father loves you will increasingly set you free to walk without shame, before God and with other people. Though shame restrains people from sin under the law, in Christ it no longer holds any purpose.

Because sin was consumed in Jesus on the cross, there is absolutely no condemnation or guilt for anyone who lives in him. You can taste this miracle of the cross every day. Now you can be with your Father just as you are, still in the process of transformation, and not have to hide anything. You can share with him your darkest secrets as you learn from him how to walk free of them. He knows you cannot fix yourself and only waits for you to recognize it and invite his help.

As he teaches you how to walk shamelessly with him, you'll also discover yourself walking shamelessly in the world. Having been bullied by shame all of your life, often without even recognizing it, you will be amazed at how much your life will change in its absence

It's an incredible gift that Dallas Willard painted in *The Divine Conspiracy*:

> *Would you like to have no need for others to praise you, and would you like not to be paralyzed and humiliated by their dislike and condemnation? Wouldn't you also like to have a strength and understanding that enables you genuinely and naturally to bless those who are cursing you—or cheating you, beating you out on the job, spitting on you in a confrontation, laughing at your religion or culture, even killing you?*

Those who are no longer influenced by shame can finally live authentic lives—the same outside as they are inside. It is a tremendous relief to be known exactly for who you are, allowing people to know both your strengths and your weaknesses. Shame-free people champion reality over image, sincerity over pretentiousness, and honesty over deceit. Admittedly there is a cost to living authentically in a broken world as others try to take advantage of you. But no one I've met who has done so would go back to the land of pretense.

OF NO REPUTATION

I have been a slave to my reputation almost my entire life, and it has been an oppressive burden. I first saw it weakening in my life in a conversation with a friend. She had asked me to write her a letter explaining my role in mediating a dispute between her and her business partner. They had begun the business out of their close friendship and now they could no longer work together. They couldn't agree on how to split up the business and asked for my help. I told them at/the outset we probably couldn't find a resolution we both thought fair, but we perhaps could find one in which they both felt equally cheated. A few hours of piecing together various options finally brought a solution.

Then, some six months later, she called me to say that her former business partner was telling her friends how she had been cheated out of the business. She wanted me to write a letter to prove the other woman a liar.

"I am willing to do that, Jill," I said on the phone, "but let me give you something to consider first. This may be an opportunity for you to die to your reputation." As the words came out of my mouth I remember cocking my head in surprise that I had said them.

For the previous four years I had also been the victim of some rumors spread about me and my family by those who wanted to discredit my ministry. I had often prepared responses to the lies that were being told, but each time God had prevented me from mailing them. "I want you to give up serving your reputation and trust it to me," was all he would tell me. I remembered that Jesus made himself of no reputation. It was the most painful season of my life. How could I encourage anyone toward a similar process?

But that morning it dawned on me how much the past four years had worked the Father's freedom into my life. If people misunderstood my ministry or believed lies about me, that was God's business, not mine. Mine was to simply do what he asked without the horrible need to defend myself and make sure other people liked me in the process. Now I could enjoy the fruits of his freedom.

I wanted Jill to have the same thing, though she was shocked by my offer. I told her my story and finished with these words: "Jill, as long as you have to guard your reputation, you are the slave of anyone who chooses to lie about you. Those who know you well enough won't need a letter, and those who don't won't believe it anyway."

I never wrote the letter, and Jill got to discover the incredible joy of living free of other people's opinions. I know it was painful, but when you know the Father loves you completely and that your reputation is secure in his hands, you will never again have to appeal for the approval of others.

That freedom not only will be one of the greatest blessings of the journey, but it is also the key to loving other people the way you've been loved yourself.

> *To him who is able to keep you from falling and to present you before his glorious presence without fault and with great joy—to the only God our Savior be glory, majesty, power and authority, through Jesus Christ our Lord.*
>
> —JUDE 24-25

For Your Personal Journey

Ask God how shame-based behaviors are manifesting themselves in your relationship with him. Look for him to identify where boasting, blaming, gossip, self-pity, and worrying about what others think are causing you to live to shame instead of living to him. Also ask him to reveal to you all the places where covering up for shame hurts your relationships with others. Ask God to draw you close enough to him so that you will no longer need to live in bondage to shame.

For Group Discussion

1. Share some of the ways you see shame working in your life.

2. How do you cover up for it?

3. How would your life and fellowship together be different if you cared what the Father thought of you more than what anyone else thought?

4. We have all heard the tapes of shame playing in our heads. Take a few moments to identify some of the things God wants you to know about the way he thinks of you.

21

Grace does not exist to make us successful. God's grace exists to point people to a love like no other love they have ever known. A love outside the lines.

MIKE YACONELLI, *DANGEROUS WONDER*

In Exactly the Same Way

HE DIDN'T KEEP IT TO HIMSELF. It might have been impossible—even for God! To hold something so beautiful for himself was unthinkable.

He had enjoyed it forever in the divine relationship of Father, Son, and Spirit. He wanted to share it so much that he made a universe to house those he would invite to share it with them.

Genuine love is like that. Part of reveling in its delights is to share it with others. When you really touch it, just try to contain it, if you can. If God didn't, how do you think you'll pull it off?

The earliest believers transformed by the cross couldn't,

even when they were being beaten with whips or battered with stones. When they were commanded to silence, they responded, "We cannot help speaking about what we have seen and heard" (Acts 4:20).

They had been touched by the greatest force in the universe and they were unable to keep it in, even when they knew it would cost them dearly. Such is the nature of God's love. As I said at the outset, there is nothing more powerful in all the world, and once you've experienced God's kind of love, there will be no way for you to keep it to yourself.

THE WELLSPRING OF LOVE

I'll have to admit that I grew up viewing love as an onerous chore. Loving others meant I had to be nice to them, even when I didn't want to. Lacking compassion, I still thought I had to act compassionately at least toward other believers.

Trying to share God's love with the world was a bit more confusing and often embarrassing. I and many of my fellow believers knew we were supposed to share the gospel with others, but often we talked about them as enemies meriting God's judgment. Most attempts to share God's love were driven by our feeling condemned if we didn't.

Because our motives lay more with our needs than theirs, we weren't really loving them. That was probably more obvious to them than it was to us. Instead of feeling loved, they felt exploited by those who wanted to get another notch on their belts.

Jesus didn't call us to convert the world but to love others the way we've been loved. As long as we act out of obligation, they will know our attempts to share with them serve only ourselves. But he also knows that we cannot love effectively if we have not been loved extravagantly. That may seem selfish, but until we trust our Father to care for us, we will constantly use the people around us to meet our needs.

The unfolding of love in our lives can begin only with the wellspring of love, the Father himself! "This is love: not that we loved God, but that he loved us and sent his Son as an atoning sacrifice for our sins" (1 John 4:10). Once we experience love as God defines it, we will not be able to keep from sharing it with others as it has been shared with us.

Where God is generous with you, you can be generous with others. Where God affirms your worth in him, you won't seek its substitute with others. Where you know God overlooks your flaws, you'll overlook them in others.

Jesus left us with one command: to love one another as we have been loved. Paul even placed love on a higher plane than spiritual knowledge, noting that knowledge can easily puff us up whereas love will build up others (see 1 Cor. 8:1). He thought it absurd that believers would trample those for whom Christ died over disputes about what foods to eat or what days to celebrate. But it happened in his day and through the course of history because we've made Christianity more about doctrine than love.

HEALTHY RELATIONSHIPS

You will soon find that your security in God's love and your awareness of his unlimited patience with you will redefine the other relationships in your life.

Instead of demanding that others conform to what you think is right, you will find yourself letting others have their own journey. By no longer manipulating them to what you think is best, you can allow them the same freedom God gives you. You will let them choose their own course based on nothing but the clarity of truth as they understand it and the willingness of their conscience. It is the task of the Holy Spirit, not you, to convict.

Instead of despising people who are broken by sin, you will be touched by the depth of bondage that holds them captive. You will also see better how the Father responds to them and then know how you can as well. Sometimes that means you'll stand back and let the consequences of sin take their course as the father did with his prodigal son. At other times it means you'll jump into the mess with them and help them find God's way out.

Instead of saying what you think people want to hear, you'll look for ways to be gently honest with them. Human love seeks people's comfort at the expense of truth. God's love seeks people's comfort in the midst of truth. He doesn't avoid the difficult moment or hold his peace just to be nice. As you experience that in your own relationship with him, you'll find yourself unable to be disingenuous with people.

Finally, by looking to God as the resource for our needs, we will find ourselves not overloading our friendships with expectations that are easily disappointed. By vesting all of our hope in God's ability to meet our needs, we will not need to force our friends to do it. I know God will often use other believers to extend his gifts and graces to me, but now I also know I don't get to choose the vessel he uses. In other words, I always look for how God is revealing himself to me through other believers, but I don't trick myself into thinking it has to come from the specific person I want him to use.

Disappointed expectations destroy relationships because we look to others in ways God wants us to look to him. Such expectations set us up for enduring frustration. However, when we give up our expectations of people, we'll find God uses some of the most unlikely people to lend us a hand. Our frustration will yield to gratefulness whenever and however God uses others to touch us or us to touch others.

A SAFE HARBOR

Instead of trying to fix people in crisis, love will call us to graciously lend them our support. We will be able to offer insights as fellow strugglers, not experts with pat answers. Then we will be safe places for people to be encouraged in their trials, to discover what it means to rely on God in the midst of it.

People who serve the illusion of a demanding God will be unwittingly destructive to people in pain. When I thought I had to work so hard to earn God's acceptance, I thought loving people meant I had to push them to do so as well. When someone came to me in crisis, I would tell them what they were doing wrong and encourage them to try harder. No wonder people in pain shied away from me.

I discovered that a few years ago as I was sitting in a roomful of people going through some very painful life experiences: lost jobs, family crises, desperately ill relatives, chronic diseases, and drug dependencies. Thinking out loud, I observed that it seemed to be a tough time for God's people. I noted that a few years earlier, most believers I knew were living the bliss of the American dream—stable families, healthy children, rising incomes.

Knowing glances shot around the room. "Should we tell him?" someone finally asked.

"Tell me what?"

"Back then you were not a safe person for people who were hurting. You had an answer for everything, and it usually added to people's feelings of condemnation and inadequacy. But the difficulties you experienced in the last few years have changed you. People sense your compassion and your trust that the Father will sort it out with them in his time."

I'll admit their observations embarrassed me, but if all the pain I'd gone through opened that kind of door for others, I can truly say it was worth it. But again, this is nothing I set out to change. Somehow, some of the patience God had poured into me had splashed out onto others without my notice.

I am amazed at what love will call people to do, and they won't even think it a sacrifice. Recently I met a woman from the Midwest who had been divorced when her ex-husband told her he was gay, that he had AIDS, and that he wanted to live with his partner. A few years later as the disease progressed, she felt compassion for her former husband and felt God wanted her to help care for him as the disease worsened.

She did just that. With her husband's permission she moved back in, not as wife but as nurse, and cared for him as the disease progressed. I can't imagine what it took for her to give of herself in this way. I don't think her obedience should become a standard for others, but she talked about it as one of the greatest experiences of her life. Before he died, her husband and his partner came to repentance and faith. What's more, after her former husband's death, she stayed on to take care of his former partner as he died. While she was doing that, other AIDS patients came to the door and asked for help. During the next decade she cared for more than sixty other patients and watched them all come to faith. Today she's converting an abandoned hospital to extend that care and travels the world helping people with AIDS and those who seek to care for them.

Love will take you further than law ever will, and what's more, you'll do it reflecting the very love you've received from Jesus.

THE EXCELLENT WAY

Without God's love filling our hearts, we'll end up hurting people despite our best intentions. For years I've heard of congregations doing "Jericho marches" around property that was needed to expand the facility to reach the neighborhood more effectively for the kingdom. I heard one pastor telling how one of their next-door neighbors sold them the property they needed after the congregation went out on a Sunday evening and marched, singing and praying that the owners would sell.

A few years later I got a look from the other side of those curtains. Our new neighbors were not Christians and let us know in no uncertain terms that they didn't want that "Jesus stuff" crammed down their throats. We assured them we would not. As we got to know them better we found out why. Their previous home had been located next to a church facility, and according to them the people there had been obnoxious in their attempts to make them move. They parked in their driveway, trampled their flowers, and one night even marched around the house chanting. They were an elderly couple and it had scared them half to death.

They had held their ground for many years thereafter, unwilling to give in. When they finally did move, they were embittered at how they had been treated and had rejected any sense of God's reality.

Over the course of the next thirteen years, however, we got to know them, mostly by taking them their mail when it had mistakenly ended up in our box. They mentioned one day how much they appreciated an article I'd written for the local paper, and our conversations more frequently turned to spiritual things. They were interested but still cautious.

Do you know what finally opened the door? One day I found out they were too ill to get their paper anymore and had to wait until the evening when their son would come over and get it for them. I told them I'd be happy to get theirs every morning when I got mine. For the next four years, until we moved, it was our family project. It wasn't any big deal to us and yet it touched them deeply.

I did get to share the life of Jesus with them and was even asked to preside at the husband's funeral when he passed away. They were not "missionary projects" to us, they were friends and neighbors whom we cared about.

God's kind of love is really the most powerful force in the universe. No wonder Paul said that to really love as God loves will fulfill every bit of the law without our even trying. Jesus said the same thing. "If anyone loves me, he will obey my teaching" (John 14:23).

I know that can be taken two ways, and for most of my life I've followed the wrong one. I used to think Jesus was saying if I really loved him I would keep all of his commands, as if my keeping would prove my loving. But the rest of his actions and teachings make that an untenable interpretation. What he's saying is that if we get the loving right, the keeping will take care of itself. Those who love him as they are loved will find themselves following him wherever he leads. That's also what Paul was saying when he said love will fulfill the whole law.

The difference is critical, for it determines where we'll invest our efforts—in keeping or loving. We know our best efforts at keeping will never be enough, but the transformation that love brings to our lives will help us live like Jesus in the world.

That's why he told us to love exactly the same way he loves us.

Until we know he does, we can't.

Once we fully know he does, we can't help but do the same.

> *A new command I give you: Love one another. As I*
> *have loved you, so you must love one another. By this*
> *all men will know that you are my disciples, if you love*
> *one another.*
>
> —JOHN 13:34–35

For Your Personal Journey

Realize that loving others is the overflow of being loved.
Wherever you see your life being given away to help others,
rejoice at what God has worked in you. Wherever you see your
love lacking toward others, ask God to take you to deeper levels of his love. Let him show you where you have expectations
of others that prevent you from loving them freely and let him
set you free.

For Group Discussion

1. Share together some of the best moments when God
   expressed his love to you through another believer. What
   made it special to you?

2. Talk about some of the things that make relationships
   helpful and what makes them harmful.

3. Where should our focus be if we don't find ourselves compassionately involved with people around us?

4. If you're a group that meets regularly together, ask God over
   the next couple of weeks if there is a specific way your group
   might express God's love to someone. Don't think of a pro-
   gram to start here unless he tells you clearly to do that, but
   rather think in terms of something practical you can do to
   bless someone without manipulating him or her.

22

Since God offers to manage our affairs for us, let us once and for all hand them over to His infinite wisdom, in order to occupy ourselves only with Himself and what belongs to Him.

J. P. DE CAUSSADE (C. 1700)

The Prayer God Always Answers

HIS TIME OF TEACHING about his Father's kingdom had drawn to an end. There would be no more opportunity to hold a leper in his hands or sit in Mary's home in Bethany and talk of his Father's wonders, at least not in this body, not in the way he had grown accustomed.

He had returned to Jerusalem for his final visit. Days away from yielding himself to those who sought to kill him, his heart was deeply troubled. He stood on the threshold of the greatest act of love and trust our world would ever behold, but he knew in doing so he would be consumed.

What should he do? Would he trust his Father's love and continue the journey, or would he cut it short in a moment of weakness and beckon angels to set him free?

Perhaps the most powerful lesson Jesus taught his disciples about prayer began by polling how they thought he should pray: "What shall I say? 'Father, save me from this hour'?"

Perhaps there were nods around the circle as they all acknowledged how good that sounded to them. That's how we're used to praying. In moments of trial and pain, it is natural even for the nonbeliever to cry out for help: "Save me, God! If you get me out of this I will serve you forever."

His disciples understood that prayer well enough, but Jesus wanted them to learn a better way. Even when it was his life at stake, Jesus was tuned to a better frequency. "No, it was for this very reason I came to this hour." What he wanted personally wasn't in the picture. He was focused elsewhere—on the purpose that transcended his personal happiness.

Then he prayed the prayer he wanted them to hear: "Father, glorify your name!" (John 12:27).

In this brief exchange you learn everything you will need to know about prayer and what it means to follow God in this life. For in every situation you'll ever encounter, you will be offered two options in prayer: "Father, save me," or "Father, glorify your name!" One will lead you to frustration and disillusionment, the other to the greatest wonders in God's heart.

WHATEVER YOU ASK?

Jesus' teaching about prayer seemed to be incredibly simple: ask for whatever you wish and be assured that the Father will give it to you.

It gets complicated only when our experience with prayer falls short of this ideal. Why would he tantalize us with such outlandish promises only to leave us disappointed in so many of the things for which we ask?

It's not so difficult to understand why he would ignore our

more selfish requests. Even his disciples had to learn that the power of prayer was not for their selfish agendas. Instead of calling down fire from heaven as James and John had asked for, Jesus taught them that such ideas came from the wrong place. And when they asked him to grant them seats on his right and left in heaven, he told them they weren't his to give and that in his Father's house there was noplace for anyone to set themselves over anyone else.

Jesus never intended prayer to be the way we manipulate God to do what we think is best. If you look carefully at Jesus' simple statements about prayer, you will see that they are set in the midst of our participating in what God is doing. While we are invited to make any request of God we like, the prayers that move God's hand are those that grow out of our trust in who he is and what he is doing.

I wonder what my life would be like now if God had given me half the things for which I've asked him. I know I would have been giddy with delight in the short term, but I would have had no idea of the hurt my selfish requests would have caused. And how would I have come to know him as my loving Father if I treated him like my genie in a bottle?

It's far more difficult to understand why our prayers for other people in pain and misery go unanswered. Was Peter responding in any way less than love when he forbade Jesus to go to Jerusalem to face his executioners? I think not. Yet his entreaty was met with the harshest rebuke, as Satan's words to keep Jesus from his mission.

Peter didn't understand God's higher purpose in the cross Jesus would suffer. For God to have answered his prayer, he would have aborted the very act that would save Peter from himself. "You do not have in mind the things of God, but the things of men" (Matt. 16:23). Peter didn't understand that his concern simply gave voice to Satan's attempt to discourage Jesus in his obedience to his Father.

It was a "save me" prayer, rising more out of fear than God's love, and like most "save me" prayers, it resisted God's purpose rather than served it.

"FATHER, GLORIFY YOUR NAME"

We were made for this!

When God fashioned the first humans, he designed them body, mind, and soul so they could participate in his glory and share in his pleasure.

If you've ever known that glory, either just sitting in his presence communing with him or having just seen him use you to reveal himself to someone else, you know what I'm talking about. At such moments it seems time itself stands still. Waves of joy sweep across you, and you feel so incredible that if you were made just for that one moment, your life would have had a wealth of meaning. "I was made for this."

And you were.

Jesus knew that about himself. Faced with two choices, "Father, save me!" or "Father, glorify your name," he chose the latter. He knew the only real glory existed in fulfilling the Father's purpose in his life regardless of the circumstances. As much as he might have dreaded the agony of the cross, he knew he had come into the world for that moment.

"Father, glorify your name."

This is the prayer the Father always answers. "Father, may the purpose for which you have created me and placed me where you have in the world be fulfilled completely." It is the prayer that disarms our self-interest and asserts our trust that the Father who made us and who loves us so deeply knows us better than we know ourselves.

We make this choice not one time for our entire lives, but in the immediacy of each situation we face. When I didn't get the job I wanted, the raise I deserved, or the medical report I hoped for: "Father, save me!" or "Father, glorify your name."

We face it when we're the subject of malicious gossip or the object of someone's selfish act: "Father, save me!" or "Father, glorify your name."

We confront it when we face people in need, the opportunity to speak the truth where it will cost us, or when we can take up the cause of the powerless: "Father, save me!" or "Father, glorify your name."

We engage it when the dark storm surrounds us, and when trials overwhelm us: "Father, save me!" or "Father, glorify your name."

A DAILY CHOICE

It's not the words you use that matter here, but the cry of your heart. Choose to save yourself, and you will find yourself resisting God when you don't even mean to. You'll end up praying against the very things God is using to transform you or the ways he'd rescue you. You'll miss him because they won't look like the thing you want.

I've got to be honest. I have spent most of my life praying "save me" prayers. I didn't always know that's what I was doing, but simply thinking that God would want the best for me defined my terms.

But God has taught me again and again in this journey that he knows best about everything. The way I would solve my problems and help other people would do more damage to us all than he would allow. When he denied me the thing I wanted, it was because he had a better way not only to deal with my circumstance but to change me in the process. In almost every situation it seems that what God is doing is the opposite of what I would do.

When he wanted to teach me to trust him more, I prayed he would fix things so I wouldn't have to.

When he wanted to lead me into the fullest participation of what he made me to be, I prayed he would just make me happy.

When he wanted to change my character so I would represent his heart to others, I wanted him to leave me the way I was and not allow me to be caught in situations where the "old Wayne" would surface.

I'm so glad he won, more often in spite of my prayers than because of them. I want him to continue to win, I really do. I want him to use everything in my life to shape me to be more like him so that he can fulfill in me the purpose for which he made me.

"Glorify your name."
In all of us, now until the end of the age.
And for eternity beyond.
Amen.

> *In him we were also chosen . . . according to the plan*
> *of him who works out everything in conformity with*
> *the purpose of his will, in order that we . . . might be*
> *for the praise of his glory.*
> —EPHESIANS 1:11–12

For Your Personal Journey

Review the things you are currently praying about. Which prayers are "Save me" prayers and which are "Glorify your name" prayers? Which serve your desires and which result from your understanding of God's purpose in the situations you're in? Ask him to reveal to you every day what his purpose is in the circumstances you face and pray for that purpose's continued unfolding as he draws you closer to himself.

For group discussion

1. Give examples from Scripture and from your own life of "Save me" prayers.

2. Now give examples of "Father, glorify your name" prayers.

3. Can you think of a time in your life when you prayed for the exact opposite of what you wanted because you felt God's purpose would be fulfilled by it? Share about that.

4. If some in your group are open to share some of the things they're praying about, ask God to show you together what his purpose is and how it will best be served by your prayers.

5. Pray for God to be glorified in your lives as the journey unfolds in the days ahead.

23

The mind of a Pharisee thinks truth is more important than love, but Jesus showed us that love is the most important part of truth.

ADAPTED FROM DON FRANCISCO'S PHARISIATIS TEST

Living Loved

OF COURSE, NOTHING IN THIS BOOK has any value if it is just an intellectual argument, or if it only spawns a theology of God's love. It has meaning only if you can learn how to live loved—to awaken to each new day confident that the Father delights over you like a parent over his newborn child.

I could go on and on with other implications of what it means to live in God's love, and how it revolutionizes everything about the way we think or live. But I think the picture is clear enough now, and you'll be able to recognize the pathway and follow it wherever your Father wants to take you. Believe me, this is a life far better lived than it is read or talked about.

I've spent twelve years mining the width and breadth of the Father's affection, and my life in him grows deeper and richer as the months go by. I keep discovering just how incredible he is and how freely I can live when I'm confident of his affection for me. I've seen him change so many things in my life this way, and yet I feel as if I'm just beginning.

You will enjoy far more the process of discovering how he wants to live in you than to just keep reading more on the subject. This is a life we can all live. If you have already tasted of that reality before you read this book, you probably already know how to begin living in his love. If so, go for it!

There may be others who have been captured by the message of this book but who still feel that they haven't the foggiest idea how they can live in his affection. Intellectually you may agree with the idea that God has affection for you, but it isn't something you've experienced firsthand. In fact, you may feel quite empty spiritually and unsure where to turn. You may not feel as if you know enough to give it a go yourself, but the fact is you never will. The day to start is today, and the time is right now.

Living in God's affection is not difficult because it is too complex for most, but because it is far simpler than most folks can believe. Let me offer you a few thoughts that might help you move ahead.

HIS WORK, NOT YOURS

Don't assume that this life is lived out of your intellect or your emotions. While both are important parts of your journey, the life I'm talking about begins in a personal revelation of the Father's love for you and the work his Son accomplished on the cross. I've tried to describe it as well as I can in this book, but words won't do it justice. Living in his affection requires a deeper revelation than that, where the eyes of your heart are opened to see into his reality.

I can't make this happen for you, so I won't even try.

You can't make it happen for you either, so please don't waste time by trying.

What you can do is simply ask him to show you the depth

of his love for you and a revelation of what the cross of Jesus accomplished. He seems to love doing this more than anything else he does, and he's been doing it with people through the whole course of history.

If you came into a room where a two-year-old child was playing and wanted to have a relationship with that child, who would have to make that happen? Would it be the child? Of course not! To forge a relationship with that toddler, you would be the one to do it. He'll have to respond, of course, but you would take the initiative. You would find a way to meet him at his level and you would engage him in things that interest him as you draw him into a relationship.

The same is true with God. He is further above you than you are above a two-year-old. He will take the initiative at your invitation. Simply ask him to begin to reveal to you how much he loves you, and he will take it from there. Don't just ask him once and wait for the sky to fall or your heart to explode. Keep focusing on him each and every day, regularly looking to him and for ways he'll make himself known to you.

LIVING WITH EYES WIDE OPEN

Jesus promised us that he was the Way to know the Father and that he would come to us so we could experience what real life is in him. As you ask him to show himself to you, live with your eyes wide open, looking for ways in which Jesus is making himself known to you. No one can tell you when or how you will encounter him, but there are some specific places he said we could look for him.

Jesus said he would be with us always, and he modeled in his own life how valuable it was to take regular time away from the crush of life to spend time with the Father. I'm not talking about the discipline of a daily devotional here, because that can easily become a rote chore and only frustrate you even more. Rather, it would simply help if you would find some regular time to just let your heart be before him. Where might that be for you? On a daily walk or a drive to work? In a special corner of your house where you find a bit of peace? It could be in the shower or in bed at night before you go to sleep.

Just ask him to make himself known to you in whatever way he desires. Don't add your expectations to that or you'll be looking for something, rather than Someone. At some point you'll recognize his presence with you with ever-increasing familiarity. It may be just the awareness that you are not alone in the world, hearing that still, small voice, or recognizing a sudden stroke of wisdom. Though you can't produce any of this in your own strength, without the quiet moments that are open to him, it is easy to miss him.

God is also invested in the Scriptures themselves. Spend some time there looking for him and his wisdom about issues that are on your mind. I encourage people to start with the Gospels and read them again and again, for months perhaps, until Jesus becomes a real person for them. If you're having trouble understanding his love, read through Romans 4–8 or the book of Galatians or Colossians. Let the words sink into your heart as he makes himself real in them.

Keep your eyes out for a community of faith to share your journey with. I don't necessarily mean the congregation meeting at the corner. It may simply start with older brothers or sisters who are growing in their own relationship with God. Listen to the things they're discovering and ask them for help when you grow weary or confused. Just make sure they are people who are growing in that affection themselves and not those locked into the demands of guilt and performance. Let them encourage you, but don't look to them for all the answers. Keep looking to Jesus as your older Brother and Guide on this journey.

And don't forget, you can find him in those who are not believers. Jesus said that as we serve "the least of these," we are engaging him. Look at how he might want to take expression through you, not in guilt-induced obligations, but in simple ways he will give you to love others around you.

RELAX

Just know that you do not control how this new relationship with God unfolds. I've told people who begin this journey to not lose heart if they don't see anything or hear anything for a year or two. I know that sounds like a long time, but I want them to relax. The pressure to make something happen in a day or two, or even a month or two, is a great deterrent to letting this relationship unfold. It rarely takes two years, but by getting the pressure off to produce it, you'll be able to see his hand so much more easily.

Why does it take time? The revelation of the Father's affection is not a matter of rubbing a magic lamp and suddenly he appears. Rather, God often has to untangle some things in you to help you see him. Even if this process takes months, it's not because he is waiting to see how sincere you are; it's because he is working deep inside you to sort out those things that crowd him out of your heart and set your focus on your own efforts or your own failures.

Sometimes that means sorting out your disappointments with him. The more you have tried to live religiously toward God, the more often you've probably been disappointed when he didn't do things you expected him to do. It might be unanswered prayer or allowing a painful experience in your life. Residual anger at him and feelings of betrayal will cloud your eyes to his presence.

Would it be best to ignore your disappointments, then? Absolutely not! It is far better to present your frustrations and disappointments to him. Bring them to the light. Talk about them in his presence. Ask him to show you a love bigger than your misunderstandings of him and watch as he sets you free from them. It won't happen overnight, but over time those misunderstandings will yield to an emerging reality that though this Father doesn't keep you from all trouble and danger in this life, he is with you through them and can even redeem you out of them to shape your love for him and your compassion for others in their pain.

All you need to do is look to him continually, ask him to help you recognize what he is already doing in your life and already whispering in your heart. The quest here is not to get God to act toward you, but for you to begin to recognize how he already is.

LETTING GUILT DIE

If you've tried to serve God religiously in the past, one of the things God will want to wrestle out of your hands is responding to him out of guilt and fear. If you have sought to appease those by doing things for him that you think will earn his favor, this won't be an easy road to walk. But until God disconnects you from the guilt and fear that drive your own performance, you will miss his love for you.

How do you let guilt die? Endure it in his presence. I know that doesn't sound like much, but it will be enough. Stop doing what you do because you'll feel bad if you don't. When you feel guilt and condemnation roll over you like a late-afternoon thunderstorm, simply acknowledge that it is there and offer it to God. Recognize that God doesn't use fear to manipulate you to act for him; therefore, don't give fear a place in your life by doing what it demands of you.

This will be hard in the early stages. You may resist for a time, and then be so overwhelmed by guilt, either internally or from what others put on you, that you will go ahead and act on it anyway. Believe me, it's not the end of the world. Just come back to Jesus when you realize it. Tell him about your struggle and ask him to set you free from it. Our intellect and emotions have so long been manipulated by guilt and our desire to appease a God we think we've failed that it is easier to believe the lies of guilt than his words of affection. Keep coming to him, and you'll learn how to resist the guilt and embrace the affection, and then you'll discover how much guilt has distracted you from knowing him.

It will also help if your touch with the body of Christ reinforces the wonder of Father's affection and disdains the use of guilt and fear to motivate people. This may not be easy to find because so many times it is easier to motivate people out of guilt than it is to help them live in the Father's love. But those voices are out there. It may be in a friend or two that God gives you, or some books you can read, or teachings or podcasts that can reinforce the Father's love for you.

FOLLOW HIM

I don't think there has been a time since the Middle Ages when the practice of Christianity was so at odds with what it means to live in the life of Jesus. One can be a good Christian by embracing its doctrines, its rituals, and its ethics without ever knowing him. Jesus did not come to start a new religion, he came to break the power of them all by inviting us to follow him and live in the reality of his love for us.

Just remember, life in Christ has more to do with following a person than it does following the rules. As you turn your heart toward him, you'll begin to recognize his voice in your conscience leading you. Follow him, not in the anxiety-ridden fear that you'll make him angry, but in the security that no one loves you more and that he is rooting for you.

So many have misunderstood Jesus' words: "If you obey my commands, you will remain in my love." He wasn't saying that we earn his love by keeping his commands, but rather that as we follow him we'll get to live in the fruit of his love. The prodigal son living in the pigpen was no less loved by his father, but he was not living in reality of that love. As long as we trust our wisdom above God's love, neither will we.

His invitation is for us to come and live as loved as we already are. Take the risk to discover that, and you'll never be disappointed. He knows best about everything and there is no situation in which he cannot work his glory into your life. As you watch him do that in your life, it will become much easier to follow him. Your trust in him will grow, and astounding transformations will occur in your life.

You'll notice it in the most surprising ways as, over time, your own thoughts, ideals, and actions gradually shift to reflect his. You'll catch yourself responding in situations totally differently from how you've responded in the past. You'll find yourself thinking, *I'm not like this*. And yet you are. You always have been, it's just that your life was distorted and twisted by a broken relationship with the Father who has always loved you more than you can possibly conceive.

That is the joy of this journey—a restored relationship with the Father who made you and a transformed life that allows you to live free even in this broken age. I can think of no better place to end than with the words of Peter as translated by Eugene Peterson in *The Message*. I have found the truth in this Scripture to be a beacon that invites me ever onward and closer to him:

> *Since Jesus went through everything you're going through and more, learn to think like him. Think of your sufferings as a weaning from that old sinful habit of always expecting to get your own way. Then you'll be able to live out your days free to pursue what God wants instead of being tyrannized by what you want.*
> —1 PETER 4:1–2, The Message

For Your Personal Journey

Go and live this life in the peace and joy of Jesus. Awaken to each new day certain of his love for you and ask him for help wherever you need it. Then listen and do your best to follow him each day. You will find this life richer and deeper than you ever thought imaginable.

For Group Discussion

No more questions here. Just share with one another how this chapter helped you see the next step Jesus might have for you on your journey.

Acknowledgments

Thank you, Kevin Smith, David Boan, and John Yates of Australia, for pulling me aside and showing me a more excellent way. Your insights on the cross revolutionized my appreciation for Father's love and helped me understand how Jesus' church can really share his life together.

Thank you, Dave and Donna Coleman of Visalia, for enriching my life and this book with the lessons you've learned and being patient with me as I went through a similar process.

Thank you, Bob Blasingame and Scott and Sandi Tompkins, for contributing your expertise to the specific content of the first publication of these pages. And to Kate Lapin, copy editor extraordinaire, and Julie Williams, beloved daughter and office manager, for cleaning up this mess and getting it ready for publication.

The cover art and interior design reflect the artistry of my good friend Dave Aldrich of Aldrich Design (aldrichdesign .com) in Rhode Island, who has been a blessing to me in so many ways and on so many projects. Dave, you're a wonderful friend and colaborer.

Thank you, dear friends in and around my former hometown of Visalia, California, for all the ways you have loved me, stood by me, and shared my journey. And thank you, too, to the many explorers I have met from all over the world who are on a similar journey to discover the depths of God's love and how to live in the joy and simplicity of being his beloved children in the earth.

About the Author

Wayne Jacobsen directs Lifestream Ministries and travels the world teaching on themes of intimacy with God and relational church life. He was a longtime contributing editor to *Leadership Journal* and is the author of *In My Father's Vineyard*, *Authentic Relationships*, *So You Don't Want to Go to Church Anymore* (coauthored with Dave Coleman), and *Tales of the Vine*. Wayne cohosts a weekly podcast at thegodjourney.com and also works as a trainer and mediator in public education, helping build bridges of cooperation and understanding where the issues of church and state collide. He resides with his wife, Sara, in Moorpark, California.

For further information about Wayne's travels and writings, you can contact him at:

LifeStream

lifestream.org
7228 University Dr. • Moorpark, CA 93021
(805) 529-1728
waynej@lifestream.org

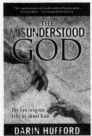